Womens Resource Center
111 Sowers St., Suite 210
State College, PA 16801

THE
FEMININITY
GAME

THE
FEMININITY
GAME

THOMAS BOSLOOPER *and* MARCIA HAYES

STEIN AND DAY/*Publishers*/New York

First published in 1973
Copyright © 1973 by Thomas Boslooper and Marcia Hayes
Library of Congress Catalog Card No. 72-96603
All rights reserved
Designed by David Miller
Printed in the United States of America
Stein and Day/*Publishers*/Scarborough House, Briarcliff Manor, N.Y. 10510
ISBN 0-8128-1545-9

ACKNOWLEDGMENTS

No book is written without the help and advice of many individuals. The experience and insights of nearly four hundred women have provided an essential source for this book. Numerous interviews were held with Rosemary Miller, Joyce McCormick, Barbara Farrell, Evelyn Ay Sempier, Elaine Erikson, Marge Burris, Patti Sligh Ver Sluis, and Caroline Friesner. Serving as consultants were Patricia Remick Packard, Neva Langley Fickling, Winifred Colton, Jane Bernot, Marilyn Ramsey, Hally Beth Poindexter, Madeline Nelson, Arden Zinn, and Chrys Schoonover.

When research began, late in the nineteen-fifties, indispensable advice and encouragement came from Daniel Bergman, professor of psychology at Central College; Professor Margarete Bieber of Columbia University, archeologist; Dr. Mirra Komarovsky of Barnard College, sociologist; and the late Dr. Arthur Steinhaus of Michigan State University, physiologist.

Some of the ideas in the book were first introduced to the public by Judy Klemesrud and Robert Lipsyte of the *New York Times* and by Roz Massow of *Parade* magazine.

There were invaluable suggestions from those who read the book in manuscript—writers Rob Gannon, Tad Richards, and Norma Harrison, psychologist Mike Proujansky, and Dr. Adelaide Hawley Cumming.

Thanks also to Doug Pirinie at *Sports Illustrated*, to Micki Scott at Oberlin's Institute for the Study of Sport and Society, to John Bittner at Penn State University, and to Paul Sturgis at the School of Experimental Studies in New Paltz, New York.

Finally, our gratitude to editors Renni Browne, Michaela Hamilton, and Mary Solberg.

CONTENTS

1 Cinderella Was a Winner   15
2 Getting Sick of the Game   27
3 The Physical Bias   41
4 The Feminine Physique   55
5 Games Women Can't Play   71
6 Bloomer Girls, Tomboys, and
   Yankee Doodle Dandies   89
7 The Masculinity Rite   101
8 How the Game Began   115
9 The Psychological Bias   137
10 Achilles Incarnate   149
11 The Naked Ape Argument   161
12 Endgame   175

   Appendices   193
   Notes   203
   Bibliography   213
   Index   221

(April 7, 1928): Tennis can be so uncivilized, but Bunky adores it. Love equals nothing? I pale at the thought. So today I gave myself a healthy glow with Charles of the Ritz Honest Bronzer, transparent color that deepens my complexion to a sun-warmed richness. It worked—I looked smashing on the courts. I even let Bunky win.

March 1973 nostalgia cosmetics advertisement, the *New York Times Magazine*

A FABLE

Somewhere in the sometime between then and now lived an amoral wizard who was a whiz at behavioral psychology. His laboratory was full of ringing bells, salivating dogs, and maze-running rats; an autographed portrait of Pavlov hung on the wall.

The wizard had been tickled pink when Skinner decided to bring his daughter up in a box, and he was itching to try a similar experiment himself. So one day the wizard went cradlenapping. He returned with two infants who tested out as identical in terms of vital functions and intelligence quotients, and he decided to see how different he could make them.

There was considerable method to his madness, for the wizard was getting on in years and foresaw the day when he couldn't manage his ivory tower alone. Eventually he would need someone to oversee his affairs in wizarddom—someone aggressive, who would fight for him when necessary and make shrewd business investments. He would also need someone to manage the tower, which was always getting dusty, and to supervise his kitchen and prepare toothsome meals.

So the wizard installed the infants in adjoining rooms in the tower and set about the task of molding their lives.

Over one door he tacked up a plaque that read "boy." Over the next went a nameplate that said "girl."

Every day the wizard played with his two infants and told them how much he loved them. He would toss the boy high into the air and treat him with rough affection. He would fondle the girl, coo softly at her, and giggle whenever she smiled.

When the children were old enough to understand words, the wizard began to read them bedtime stories. He told the boy about Jack the Giant Killer, and other brave young men who had overcome impossible odds. He told the little girl about Cinderella and Snow White, whose reward for being pretty, sweet, obedient, and hardworking was a prince with lots of money.

When the children were a little older still, the wizard got them interested in toys and games. He gave the little girl dolls and toy dishes; the little boy got a football and a baseball, along with two teams the wizard conjured up for him to play with.

"Life is like a game," he told the little boy. "Sometimes you win and sometimes you lose, and gradually you get better and better at what you're doing. The best way to learn about all that is through competitive sports, where losing and winning don't matter so much. You can get very good at these sports, by trying harder every time. And when you grow up, you'll get very good at keeping ahead of your competitors and making investments."

One day the little girl got bored with her doll house and toy kitchen and ran out onto the football field. She intercepted a running pass and made a fifty-yard touchdown. "Wasn't I terrific?" she shouted at the boy. He started to smile, but the wizard materialized on the spot, wearing his most ferocious expression. "This isn't a good game for you to be playing," he told the little girl. "Aggressive, competitive behavior isn't becoming in girls; in fact it's downright unlovable. You'll never catch a prince that way."

So the little girl went back to her doll house, and that night the wizard bought her a stereo and lots of records as a reward. She listened first to a Rodgers and Hart tune about "the most beautiful girl in the world," who "picks my ties out, eats my candy, drinks my brandy" and another one about the girl "who sews her trousseau in a little blue room away upstairs." After that the wizard put on a selection from *Annie Get Your Gun* about "a doll I can carry, the girl that I marry must be."

Later on the wizard brought the girl up to date with the Rolling Stones, and she listened to a song about "a Siamese cat of a girl . . . the sweetest thing you've ever seen . . . she's under my thumb," and "she's all I'll ever want and need . . . she'll take what I dish out . . . she'll stay at home while I go out . . . she's a lady. . . ."

"What's a lady?" asked the little girl.

"That's what you are now," said the wizard. "You're a beautiful little lady, and ladies don't play rough games."

The next day in school the wizard gave a lecture in sex differentiation. "So you see," he concluded, "it is the opinion of medical science, anthropology, sociology, theology, and just about anything else you care to name that boys and girls are physically and emotionally different and therefore suited for different occupations and activities. Class dismissed."

The little boy ran out to play another game of football while the little girl and the wizard went upstairs to play checkers and bingo. Later on, he taught the girl how to chart her horoscope, throw the I Ching, and read Tarot cards. She thought these games were lots of fun.

"I thought you would," said the wizard. "You see, your life is like a game too, but it's a different sort of game, involving some strategy and lots of chance. Playing checkers and bingo and reading your horoscope are all models of your life. If you give it some thought, you can see that Cinderella is a game too. She followed the girl's rules and listened to her fairy godmother, and she hit the jackpot."

"But Mr. Wizard," said the girl. "The boy's game is just a preparation for the real game—for what he's going to do when he grows up. But you make it sound like my whole life is going to be a game."

"I suppose you could put it that way," said the wizard. "But look at all the rewards in store. You don't have to worry about initiative and competition and all that. Just be a good girl and keep playing those numbers. Someday you'll hit bingo. Believe me, I'm a good wizard, and I know what's best for you. By the way, what's for dinner?"

To show her he meant well, the wizard did a little wand-waving over the meat loaf that night and turned it into beef Wellington.

The years went by, and the boy went off to business school. The girl waited, reading a lot of romantic novels the wizard had bought her and watching old movies out of the wizard's private collection. She saw *Kiss Me, Kate*, a musical about an aggressive girl who was called a shrew until she learned to be passive, obedient, and ladylike so her husband would treat her right. The girl also saw a movie called *Billie*, starring Patty Duke, about a girl track star who gave it all up to go to the prom with a boy who couldn't run as fast as she could.

During the day, the girl vacuumed the tower, polished the crystal balls, and perfected her cooking skills. All along she had a feeling that something important was going to happen to her, but she didn't know when, and there wasn't anything she could do to make it happen.

On the day the boy graduated from business college, the wizard bought him a white five-hundred-horsepower Maserati, a Cardin suit, and a Countess Mara tie. When he arrived home for the celebration dinner, the wizard closed his eyes tight and cast a love spell.

The little girl, who was by now a lady, looked up and smiled at the boy. "Gee," she said, "you look just like a prince!"

"You look pretty good yourself," said the boy. Later, on the terrace, he told her: "You're just the kind of girl I've been looking for, so delicate and feminine. You're smart, but you don't let it show like all those college grinds. And you're a great cook. Will you marry me?"

The girl, realizing that the wizard had been right all along, gave her breathless assent. They were married a month later at a gala affair, with a catered reception for two hundred in the tower. The wizard, hospitalized with a prostate condition complicated by gout, sent his congratulations by wire.

The newlyweds lived happily for about two weeks. Then the wizard came home to convalesce in the spare bedroom, the hospital bills started coming in, and the tower roof began to leak.

"Would you please fix the roof, dear?" the girl said, over a cup of Sanka one morning. "The feather bed is soaking wet."

"Lay off, will you?" snarled the prince. "All you do is nag, nag, nag."

The wizard, overhearing the conversation, realized that things weren't working out quite as planned, but he was too tired to do anything about it and consoled himself with the thought that the arrangement was, at least, practical.

Perhaps, he thought, it would be better if he faded out of the picture entirely. And so he did.

When the girl woke up the next morning, the wizard had passed away, taking his spells with him. Looking around her, the girl realized that she hadn't hit the jackpot at all; she'd been fleeced. All she had to show for her game was a dusty old tower with a leaking roof. And on the pillow beside her, wearing the expensive pajamas, was only the boy next door.

The End

1

CINDERELLA WAS A WINNER

> Just about the most common complaint of talented women . . . is that they *can't finish things.* Partly because finishing implies being judged—but also because finishing things means being grown up. More important, it means possibly succeeding at something. And success, for women, is always partly failure.
>
> Erica Jong
> *Ms.*
> December 1972

> The game women play is men, and perhaps that leaves them free to be less involved with this one.
> "Adam Smith"
> *The Money Game*[1]

Most women are losers. Sometimes they lose through lack of opportunity; more often, they lose by choice. Even those who have the odds in their favor in terms of education, money, and intelligence—and who are competing in the most favorable feminist climate the world has seen for some three thousand years—still end up throwing the game. Women don't know how to win or how to compete, and they're programed not to try.

These are meant to be fighting words. For if women are ever to get to a point where they can do something, *really* do something, to change their lives and society, they will have to learn to win and win big. Not in imitation of men, but in full realization of themselves.

A lot has been said and written recently about unreasonable sexual roles, about the arbitrary attitudes that divide masculine and feminine natures into polar opposites, like male and female electrical plugs and outlets. It's now generally acknowledged, in theory if not in practice, that women are men's intellectual equals and deserve the same career opportunities and pay.

But for all the new laws and policies, few women—even when they make it—can stand long in the winner's circle. Women have been conditioned to fear success, and to cop out when it gets too close. The cop-out can be as glamorous as living happily ever after with a prince or an oil tycoon, as sordid as an overdose of Seconal, as selfless as sacrificing personal ambitions to the cause of sisterhood. The first alternative will be applauded, the second pitied, the last scorned. But all are viewed as the natural outcome of feminine ambition—as, in a way, they are.

The big game is fixed. Women who don't take a dive become, in society's eyes, losers in a more basic sense: neuters who have broken the rules on their home playground—the rules of the femininity game.

All women know about this game. At one time or another most have played it. And with the possible exception of lesbians and the most dedicated women's liberationists, most still do. The goal is a man and, traditionally, marriage. The sporting equipment is charm, guile, social shrewdness, clothes, cosmetics—and, underneath it all, one's own physical apparatus (hopefully 36-24-36). No holds are barred.

Deception, flattery, and manipulation are all respectable tactics. The competitors are all other eligible women, beginning, in preadolescence, with Mom.

The femininity game meets the two basic requirements of other destructive life games. It is essentially dishonest, having an ulterior motive, and it has a dramatic payoff.[2] But unlike other games classified by transactional analysts (the species of social psychiatrist who first defined life games and now referee them), the femininity game is not entirely voluntary. Women play it because the payoff—love—is too tempting to resist. For love, women are persuaded to smother their identities and their ambitions, channeling all their competitive and aggressive instincts into the game.

At some magical moment, usually determined by adolescent alterations in their bodies, girls are expected to trade in their tennis shoes for glass slippers. Like Cinderella's sisters, they struggle to fit oversized feet into tiny glass shoes. Usually they manage to squeeze them on and totter through a lifetime of discomfort, blaming themselves for the bad fit instead of the capricious cobbler, who had a passion for glass and triple-A size fours.

Only ladies can play the game, and ladies are supposed to be supportive, passive, unaggressive, even frail. The role and the game could be amusing as an occasional charade under soft candlelight. Unfortunately, it's taken very seriously by both sexes. Girls who don't play it will have a rough time with parents, friends, and teachers.

A basic rule of the femininity game is that its contestants must be prepared to lose all the other games. Men don't love women who win. This fact of life was illustrated recently in an episode of the family television series *My World and Welcome to It*. The juvenile star of the show has just finished a chess game with her father, who is accepting defeat less than graciously. Her mother calls her aside for a heart-to-heart chat. "There's a game all women play, dear," she says. "It's called getting married and living happily ever after."

"But I can beat Daddy at chess," says the girl. "You mean I have to let him win?"

"I think," says Mom, "that it would be the feminine thing to do."

Margaret Mead would call it negative reinforcement. Winning games against men elicits such a negative response that girls learn early to lose rather than face rejection—whether from boys and girls their own age, or from fathers.

"The bribe offered to the little girl by the father is love and tenderness," psychiatrist Helene Deutsch has written. "For its sake she renounces any further intensification of her activities, particularly of her aggressions."[3]

Social and parental bribes are not often subtle. At home a girl may be confronted, as was one Michigan girl, with a father who wants to exchange her baseball bat for an electric blender. Or she may beat her father at arm wrestling and be sent to a psychiatrist—which happened to the daughter of a New York YMCA executive. Or, if she goes to a Midwestern sorority-oriented school, she may find, as one student did, that "you can be a sorority girl or a track and field girl. You can't be both."

"When I was about fourteen, I was pressured into giving up sports," says Judy Mage, founder and former president of the New York Social Service Employees' Union and one-time vice-presidential candidate on the Peace and Freedom Party ticket. "I used to play street games with the boys on our block in the Bronx. But as I got older, people would just stop and stare at a girl playing, as if I were a freak. I was getting into liking boys, and wanted to be accepted. One night after a dance I got into a snowball fight with some boys. The girls took me aside later and said 'boys don't like that.' And that's when I gave up."

Betty Friedan has noted that at puberty girls drop special interests and pursue those that will appeal to boys. "Men compete for awards, and we compete for men," said a recent *Ms.* editorial.

Having been taught that "winning" means losing love, girls usually find that achievement is accompanied by anxiety. In a study conducted by Matina Horner, now president of Radcliffe College, 65 per cent of a group of women at the University of Michigan expressed anxiety over feminine success figures, equating success with a loss of femininity. At Radcliffe, students were asked to describe a hypothetical student named Anne, who is at the top of her medical school class. Nearly 75 per cent of the group pictured her as unattractive and hard up for dates. When asked what would happen to Anne when she learned about her top standing in the class, one student replied: "Anne will deliberately lower her academic standing during the next term, while she does all she can to subtly help Carl. His grades come up, and Anne soon drops out of medical school. They marry, and he goes on in school while she raises their family."[4]

No comparable study has been done on reactions to successful sportswomen, but one can assume that the negative percentages would be considerably higher. Physical prowess and the aggressive, competitive instincts that go with it are thought of as exclusively masculine qualities.

"I didn't take physical education in college, even though I love sports," says a girl who was named queen of the

Drake Relays, an annual track event in the Midwest. "I was really afraid that I would be associated with the typical physical-education majors, who were definitely mannish."

The result of this kind of pressure is that "as age increases, sports prowess increases in boys but not in girls," says Dr. John Kane of St. Mary's College, London. "A girl's performance level is deflected to other, more acceptable behavior during late adolescence." And he adds: "With society's expectations of women, it's not surprising we get the kind of women we're asking for."[5]

Women's attitudes toward competition and success are established early. Infant girls are handled differently from boys—more affectionately, more protectively. And as soon as they learn to walk, girls are *trained* differently. Sociologists John Roberts and Brian Sutton-Smith confirmed this in a cross-cultural study of 1900 elementary-school children given a variety of psychological tests and interviews. "Boys . . . are given higher achievement training," they concluded, "while girls are given more consistent obedience-and-responsibility training. These differences in socialization correspond to the general differences between adult male and female roles over the world."[6]

It doesn't stop there. Anyone who has snoozed through introductory psych knows about Skinner's boxes and Pavlov's dogs. Behavioral training has to be reinforced to be effective. And in all cultures, games and sport serve this purpose. They are not idle play but life models—dress rehearsals, as it were, for the real thing.

Competitive team sports involving displays of power and physical skill, Roberts and Sutton-Smith found, were game models for youngsters—mostly boys—whose parents encouraged achievement and success.

Games of strategy were found to mirror childhood training in responsibility. For boys, who are trained in social responsibility, strategy games are preparation for gaining a responsible position in life; games like football, which combine strategy and physical skill, are models both for social responsibility and for power.

Finally, games of chance and fortune were the choice of two groups: those children who had been strictly disciplined in obedience (a preference shared in maturity by minority and low-income groups) and girls. Discouraged from initiative and achievement, these children could only dream that their ambitions might some day be realized by chance.

Roberts, Sutton-Smith, and Robert Kozelka followed up this research on children with polls of some 7000 adults who had a variety of occupations and income levels. (The polls were conducted by Minnesota, Gallup, and Roper.) The same game preferences were indicated.

Business executives, politicians, and other men in positions of power, for instance, overwhelmingly favored games that combined strategy and physical skill. Those in professional occupations—accountants, for instance—preferred games of strategy, like poker. Men in blue-collar jobs enjoyed games of pure physical skill, such as bowling, while women (and members of ghettoized minority groups) showed an overwhelming preference for games of pure chance, or those combining strategy and chance.

It would appear then that the battle really *was* won on the playing fields of Eton. Boys train for success and power through competitive games and sports. Feminine skills and wiles are honed at the bridge table, the bingo board, and the lottery ticket window, perfected in the femininity game.

This same group of sociologists found that real-life situations have equivalents or parallels not only in games and sport but in myths. Fairy tales and other stories written to formula are really literary games which can be scored in terms of winners and losers. Ideally, they provide a way for children to experiment with winning and losing in symbolic situations.

"Desiring to beat opponents but frightened to lose," say Roberts, Sutton-Smith, and Kozelka, "the child is motivated . . . to deal with his conflict in more manageable fashion. He is attracted to a variety of expressive models. Some of these may be as vicarious as folk tales, comics, and television, and may suggest that the small participant can win . . . or that the central figure may have powers to overcome insuperable odds (Superman). . . . Through these [play] models, society tries to provide a form of buffered learning, through which the child can make . . . step-by-step progress toward adult behavior."[7]

Boys have Superman and Jack the Giant Killer; girls have Cinderella—the beautiful, unassuming, supportive drudge whose lucky number is written on the prince's shoebox. Cinderella was obviously a winner and the wicked stepsisters losers in what is essentially a vicarious game of chance. This theme—a literary form of the femininity game—pits feminine woman against unfeminine shrew, bitch, or witch. The payoff is the prince, and usually princely sums of money as well. A well-known variation is the tomboy-turned-lady plot (*Annie Get Your Gun, The Taming of the Shrew*), a sort of double solitaire in which both women and men win by playing their respective roles to the hilt.

Because the femininity game combines strategy and chance, it is an attractive alternative to real life, one which mirrors early training and offers a strong incentive—love—as reward for conforming to a stereotype. The game is self-perpetuating because the payoff depends on masking real identity. Players know they are loved not for themselves but for their roles, and few have the self-confidence necessary to break away from the game.

Another sociologist, Roger Caillois, would classify the femininity game as mimicry. "Every game [involving mimicry] presupposes the temporary acceptance, if not of an illusion . . . at least of a closed, conventional and in certain respects, fictitious, universe," he has written. "The subject plays at believing, at pretending to himself or at making others believe that he is someone other than he is; he temporarily forgets, disguises, strips his own personality in order to be another."[8]

Faced with a conflict between what she is and what she is expected to be, an ambitious, competitive, athletic girl often responds by becoming defensively aggressive and masculine in attitude. Resenting her restrictive role but lacking the self-confidence and initiative to create something else, she becomes a hostile mimic of the only success models around: men.

Occasionally, given parental support or outside encouragement, she may create a new, successful role for herself. Unfortunately, unless her mother has been an athlete or a career woman, she will find few feminine success models to imitate. At the 1972 Penn State Conference on Women and Sport, a study of elementary school students was cited in which boys listed 150 life roles they wanted to imitate. Girls could think of only 25.[9]

Most women, of course, neither rebel nor create. They play the game—sometimes pretending, sometimes even believing themselves to be something they're not. And for centuries, the game and the role requirements have been an effective way to keep women insulated from life.

Women, conditioned to the femininity game from infancy,

are expected to play for a lifetime. Society thus dooms them to perpetual childhood, playing adult as they once played house as children, dependent on husbands as they were once dependent on parents, chastised for showing initiative and independence.

Full-time gameswomen will find all sorts of subsidiary contests to occupy them after the big prize has been won at the wedding: New House, Expectant Mother, Hostess —and, more and more often, Divorce and Remarry, when the original payoff palls.

The game also creates a masculinity trap for men, who feel threatened when their wives take over roles they are expected to perform. A man's independence often hinges on his wife's dependence. "When a man is thought superior because he is a man," Florida Scott-Maxwell has written, "then woman is crippled by the inferiority she sees in him."

A woman sufficiently attractive and talented may decide to play both sides of the fence, using the game as an entree to the career world. Women have often been criticized for this, for using feminine wiles to gain power. But these tactics are the only ones most women know. Their equipment is looks and charm, which tend to erode with age, so they play the game as hard as they can in the limited time available. Their power base is men. Their opponents, unfortunately, are other women.

Women who play the game successfully find, when the crow's feet begin to track the corners of their eyes, that it's a losing proposition. At forty-five or fifty, after decades of dedication to beauty and passivity, they suddenly find themselves out of the competition, with no identity or purpose to fall back on. As Freud once put it, "The difficult development which leads to femininity [seems to] exhaust all the

24

possibilities of the individual."[10] Freud should know. He wrote part of the script.

The physical requirements of the femininity game encourage a neurotic preoccupation with physical appearance. Women are usually self-conscious rather than proud of their bodies, spending an excessive amount of time trying to improve their looks. Because men are the payoff, players tend to evaluate themselves and other women through a man's eyes. The seductively clad girls on the cover of *Cosmopolitan* and other women's magazines are models that women will presumably envy and try to emulate. When women meet for the first time, they size each other up in terms of attractiveness—not to each other, but to men.

This perspective also leads women to think of themselves and each other as objects, both to envy other women for qualities they lack and to despise them, as they often despise themselves, for the role they are playing. Because the financial and personal destiny of players so often rests on the payoff, one can expect to find jealousy and disloyalty affecting adult feminine friendships—attitudes often carried into the career world.

Women aren't *born* losers. They're brainwashed. They don't know how to win because they've been conned and coerced from infancy into believing they shouldn't try. Except for fashionable differences in dimension—from the Rubens model to Twiggy—the physical image of woman has remained the same for thousands of years. Women have succeeded in liberating their intellects, but their bodies are still in corsets. They still think of themselves as passive, nonaggressive, and supportive. And that's why, no matter how intellectually or sexually liberated they are, women continue to lose.

2

GETTING SICK OF THE GAME

I'm tired of everlastingly being unnatural and never doing anything I want to do. I'm tired of acting like I don't eat more
than a bird and walking when I want to run, and saying I
feel faint after a waltz, when I could dance for two days and
never get tired. I'm tired of saying "how wonderful you are"
to fool men who haven't got one-half the sense I've got, and
I'm tired of pretending I don't know anything, so men can
tell me things and feel important while they're doing it.

Scarlett O'Hara
Gone with the Wind[1]

Constitutional weaknesses are not to be laid at the door of
our common mother, Nature. Custom and ignorance have been
meddling so long with her legitimate operations that she may
well decline to recognize in the modern product more than
a pitiable burlesque of the model.

Marion Harland
Eve's Daughters (1882)[2]

After years of playing the femininity game, a lot of women
start climbing the walls of their little blue rooms or drinking
up all his brandy. Mental illness and alcoholism are two
major side effects of forced femininity in an age when
women's intellectual expectations have been raised to
unprecedented levels.

Told that they are equal to men, urged to take advantage of new career opportunities, women still find that social approval and economic status are assured only when they play the traditional role. And today's concept of femininity continues to be directly opposed to the qualities we admire in a successful man: competitiveness, independence, strength, and aggressive drive. A woman's dilemma could be compared to that of a novice fisherman angling for trout with a piece of twine and a bent pin. "The fish are there," says a companion, who has the best rod, reel and tackle available at Abercrombie and Fitch. "You can get them if you try hard enough."

This conflict between career expectation and social conditioning has existed for decades, but women are more aware of it now than ever before. They are surrounded by extreme stereotypes—the TV-commercial image of the perfect housewife and mother, the media-distorted image of the militant woman's libber, the spectre of the lonely divorcee—which seem to offer either/or alternatives, rewards or punishments for playing or refusing to play the game. Many women end up compromising, attempting to play in a man's world according to the old feminine rules. They take the femininity game to work with them, where they get pushed into the winner-take-all treadmill on which men are trapped. At night they come home, masks still in place, to fix dinner, vacuum the rug, and put the kids to bed.

It is no coincidence that the number of women who seek psychiatric help or are hospitalized for mental disorders is greater now than at any time in the past. In all types of hospitals and in outpatient clinics, more than twice as many women as men are admitted as psychotics, manic depressives, neurotics, or hypochondriacs; while the number of women diagnosed as paranoid or schizophrenic is about 15 per cent greater. (According to current statistics from the National Institute of Mental Health, the number of women patients admitted to general psychiatric wards increased between 1960 and 1969 from 219,950 to 259,701—four times that of male admissions for the same period, which rose from 150,630 to 160,535.)[3]

Although more men are hospitalized for alcoholism—traditionally a "masculine" affliction—women are quietly beginning to drink men under the statistical tables. The National Council on Alcoholism reports that nearly half, possibly more, of an estimated 9 million liquor-addicted Americans are women. Many are hidden alcoholics, who sip sherry while watching the afternoon soaps; others belt down three martinis at business lunches or enjoy happy-hour equality at their local pubs.[4]

And we've come a long way, baby, toward equalizing the lung cancer mortality rate. Some 35 per cent of American women now smoke, only 10 percent fewer than men—a percentage that has risen steadily in the twenty-five to forty-five age group over the past fifteen years. Despite the hazards, women are three times more likely than men to continue smoking, says the American Cancer Society. And as more female smokers reach the age when the habit's lethal effects show up, more are succumbing to lung cancer (a total of 14,100 women died from it in 1972).

The past two decades have seen a steady increase in the number of women liberated to smoke and get drunk, dubious freedoms that leave emancipated customers with hacking coughs, headaches, and habits. During the same period, the number of working women has increased too—to some 43 per cent of the total employed. But women are not increasingly gaining financial success. The percentage of women earning more than $10,000 a year remains minuscule—only

1 per cent.[5] In the past fifteen years, in fact, women's incomes have actually fallen further behind men's incomes. In 1971 a working woman grossed, on the average, only 59.5 per cent as much as the average male worker—a figure which is down by nearly 4 per cent from 63.3 per cent in 1956. (Even adjusting for a 10 per cent difference in male and female working hours, the working woman is still 34 per cent behind her male counterpart in earnings.)

Financial dependency is still the lot of most women who have children. Those who are divorced face, for the most part, dead-end, low-paying jobs. Working women who remain married usually find that they are doing two jobs, and that their career does little more than pay for a housekeeper, new appliances, and clothes. Incredibly enough, this situation is accepted by most working women—with resentment, perhaps, but without much expectation of changing it.

Marriage, a new house, and children may be enough to keep a woman preoccupied through her mid-twenties. But once the children are in school, she begins to take stock and is apt to conclude that something is drastically wrong. This is the age when fatigue, anxiety, depression, migraines, overweight, and alcoholism are most likely to become problems.

What's wrong is that a job, whether in or out of the house, isn't enough. The problem is one of completeness as a person, both psychological and physical: a total identity. Most women have forgotten who they are. Their postadolescent identities have been built on the expectations of others—parents, husbands, and children—leaving much of the real self strewn in fragments along the way.

Yet by meeting the expectations, by playing a stereotyped role, a gameswoman has gained social approval, a house, and a family. Her community standing and economic status depend on her ability to play the part expected of her. Consequently, when women finally discover they don't know who they are, they also discover that they're afraid—and, in many cases, virtually powerless—to find out.

If a woman asserts herself professionally, she is certain to be accused of competing with her husband, of being too independent, of sacrificing her children's well-being to her own selfish drives. And if her husband won't put up with it, how will she be able to earn a living and support children on a beginner's salary? She'll face a struggle for financial survival, loneliness, and continued self-doubt, and many will say that she deserves to be so punished for her behavior. How many persons, of either sex, would have the courage to face such a future? It's easier to live with yourself as a stranger.

Masculine roles, as rigid and confining as they may be, at least allow the development of a consistent and complimentary physical and psychological identity from infancy onward. Girls are given a little more than a decade of such freedom—if that—and then, at puberty, are expected to literally split their personalities. They are permitted to be intellectually and artistically precocious as adults. But at the age when boys are encouraged to become *physically* competitive and aggressive, to test their strength and physical ability, girls are asked to give up these pursuits.

"At about thirteen is the time when boys go through a real apprenticeship in violence," writes Simone de Beauvoir, "when their aggressiveness is developed, their will to power, their love for competition; and it is just at this time that the girl gives up rough games. . . . [Even] the sportswoman never knows the conquering pride of a boy who pins his opponents' shoulders to the ground. . . . In many countries . . . scuffles and climbing are forbidden, [girls'] bodies have to suffer things only in a passive manner; they must give up emerging beyond what is given and asserting themselves above other people; they are forbidden to explore, to venture, to extend the limits of the possible. . . ."⁶

"Who wants to do all that anyway?" a woman might ask. But if she had had the chance to do all that, she would have a totally different attitude toward herself and the world—and might be doing something different for a living. Unfortunately, aggression, competition, strength, and physical prowess—qualities necessary to success in this culture—are developed in men and frowned upon in women, who are graded on their social and cultural abilities.

"The competitive woman destroys something in a man," syndicated columnist June Wilson wrote in 1960, ". . . a thing called self-respect. The woman who competes with a man on his level and so destroys him may indeed create a pinnacle for herself, but it will be a tower of ridicule and a lonely spire. For only when a man stands tall can he build for woman the pedestal he yearns to put her on."⁷

Destruction, loneliness, ridicule, no more pedestals —that's competition. Who can afford it? These syndicated sentiments are not, unfortunately, out of date. Similar views have been recently expressed by Lucianne Goldberg and other antifeminists who argue that it is destructive and/or "unnatural" for women to display such qualities. The same attitude underlies the decision of Olympic officials to count the chromosomes of women athletes, who defy the feminine stereotypes by being strong and competitive—and aggressive.

"My wife isn't aggressive," yelped Johnny Carson one night, after drummer Buddy Rich had complimented her on her vivacity and aggressiveness. "She's very sweet." The word, when applied to women, connotes misplaced hostility, belligerence, and repressed sexuality rather than vigor and forcefulness.

So women turn their aggressive instincts inward, becoming passive and masochistic. Enter the backaches, headaches, and other stress-connected disorders.[8] Repressed aggression soon smolders into hostility; turned inward, it quite logically results in depression and self-destructive impulses.

Few women have positive attitudes about aggression, competition, strength, or skill. They may have been punished by parents, derided by friends, or humiliated by men for displaying these qualities, and as a result have a poor physical orientation as adults. Often they go through life feeling awkward and self-conscious, ashamed and afraid of their physical instincts because they don't conform to prevailing stereotypes.

"My parents were disgusted with me for wrestling and playing rough with boys in grade school," says a twenty-five-year-old concert pianist. "They gave me a horse so I'd stay away from boys. Later on they completed the feminization process by putting a piano in front of me."

This woman had sought psychological counseling because of intense anxiety, shyness, and the feeling that she was awkward and unfeminine. "In college," she recalls, "I once got a lot more satisfaction from a swimming coach telling me I had well-developed arm and leg muscles than from all the applause I've ever gotten at piano recitals—but I felt guilty about feeling that way."

Another musician, at forty, had taken complaints of lethargy, backaches, and anxiety to every medical center within five hundred miles of her home. Though strikingly beautiful, she thought of herself as ugly and awkward. As a child, she had loved sports and been a good basketball player and swimmer. When her parents discouraged these abilities and encouraged only her musical talent, she became an accomplished cellist and pianist.

In high school, her physical strength was a source of embarrassment. She recalls being challenged, along with other girls, to a weight-lifting contest with boys. After lifting weights the boys couldn't budge, she was ridiculed and called an "ox."

Like many other women, she now views physical strength and skill as unfeminine and associates aggressiveness with hostility and humiliation. "It never occurred to me to fight back after the weight-lifting incident," she said. "I let myself be humiliated. The strange thing is that this has carried over to the rest of my life. Whenever there's a setback, I get terribly depressed and physically immobilized—unable to lift myself out of the slump, just as I was unable to get angry at those boys who insulted me."

Experiences like this are common in the lives of girls and young women. Most often it is a brother or father who deliberately puts down an aggressive, strong girl, permanently turning her away from further exhibitions of strength or prowess. As adults, women may exercise to make their figures more desirable—but they rarely *exert* themselves the way men do.

"Physical action . . . is very difficult for women," psychologist Phyllis Chesler has written. "Conditioned female behavior is more comfortable with, is defined by, psychic and emotional self-destruction. Women are conditioned to experience physicality—be it violent, destructive or pleasurable—more in the presence of another, or at male hands, than alone. . . ."9

Conditioned to believe that passivity and masochism are normal, women have learned to expect to be hurt—and, often, to enjoy it. The late psychiatrist Abraham Maslow, who like Freud defined feminine aggression in sexual terms, theorized that aggressive women want to be raped, while what he called medium-dominance women want to be seduced. Of low-dominance women, he said, "God knows what they want."[10]

Every hurtful experience a woman has reinforces her passive conditioning, even as it destroys self-confidence and feelings of self-worth. Yet this resulting lack of confidence is considered, in traditional psychoanalytic theory, to be a normal feminine trait. Betty Friedan has recalled that Dr. Maslow spent an entire day trying to persuade her that his concept of "self-actualization—the healthiest, most self-confident and self-contained state an individual can achieve—could not be achieved by women. (To Friedan's credit, she finally persuaded him that it could.)[11]

Women, while they will act on behalf of others, find it difficult to act for themselves. In an emergency, where children or other dependents are involved, they often behave with extraordinary courage; but they do not display the same qualities when they themselves are involved. If a study were done on comparative fatality rates during disasters, one suspects that female victims would outnumber men. Of a large group of employees recently trapped in flames on the third floor of a motel, only five women and a man—a native of India—failed to save themselves by jumping from the windows. The women's bodies were found fused together in the center of the room, where they had huddled when the building collapsed. "I tried to get them out," said a fellow employee, "but they just wouldn't move."

Women are conditioned to be creatures of fate, waiting to be acted upon rather than taking action themselves. On one level, this attitude is expressed in a fear of success; on another, in reliance on luck or on addictive escapes from the paradox of identity in which they find themselves.

Fatigue is perhaps the most common physical effect of conditioned feminine passivity in later life, and doctors' calendars are crowded with the names of housewives trying to find a solution to their private energy crises.

In December 1972, the *New York Times* carried a front-page story revealing that the famous "B-12" shots so many busy people had been getting from a Park Avenue doctor to pep them up were actually a mixture of vitamins and speed. The shots were a cure-all for depression, hangovers, and anxiety—but, most commonly, for fatigue. Although the *Times* story referred primarily to "Beautiful People" who had been duped, housewives and working women in substantial numbers have fallen into the same trap. Housework is just as hard as hopping to London for dinner and Rome for the weekend—and a hell of a lot less fun.

Women are busier than anyone else. A survey by the Chase Manhattan Bank estimated that suburban mothers who cope with a house, howling children, laundry, shopping, and meals put in an average ninety-six-hour week; careerwomen who are wives, mothers, and weekend or after-work cooks, housekeepers, and hostesses put in even more. More "active" than men, women are at the same time more inactive physically. It's no wonder that they complain so frequently of exhaustion.

Phyllis Chesler has reported a 1968 comparative study between ex-mental patients and "normal" housewives which showed many behavioral parallels. "Forty-six per cent [of the normal housewives] were described as restless; 59 per cent as worn out; 60 per cent as tense and nervous; 57 per cent as 'grouchy.'" And the ex-patients, says Dr. Chesler, exhibited the same "feminine" behavior patterns: "fatigue, insomnia, pill-taking, and general 'inactivity.'"[12] In other words, more than half of the supposedly normal women behaved in a way that the others had been institutionalized for. Their normal response to an irrational feminine role could, if others so judged it, be called "insane."

For those who can't afford to shoot speed, the next best thing—according to TV commercials—is an iron supplement. "How do you do it, honey?" the tired commuter asks his radiant, elegantly coiffed wife, who has somehow made it through the daily suburban mill prior to his arrival. "I take care of myself, eat right, get lots of exercise—and take Geritol every day," she replies. "My wife," he tells the camera. "I think I'll keep her."

The odds are that a real-life housewife doesn't eat right or get much exercise and keeps knocking back the Geritol—or Excedrin, or Anacin, or whatever—like a magic potion. If she's feeling tired and run down, the last thing she thinks of doing is running around the block or playing a set of tennis, even though that might help.

"I was usually so exhausted before a concert that I had to spend the afternoon in bed," says concert soprano Helen Merritt. "When it was suggested that I get out and exercise—take a bike ride instead of a nap—I thought it was ridiculous. It never occurred to me that my love of sport and active athletic life as a teenager was connected in any way to the tremendous energy and ability I had then. I let myself go, stopping all my athletic activities during the years I was having babies and raising my family. I didn't realize that was what exhausted me."

Inactivity can lead to more than exhaustion. When young women have been highly active physically and give the activities up entirely, the effect on the muscles and skeleton is often disastrous. Stomach muscles deteriorate, no longer providing support for the spine, and back trouble usually develops.

Eileen Schauler, for years a leading diva at the New York Civic Opera Company, almost forfeited her career to physical inactivity. Though she had been athletic as a child, the demands of her musical education gradually became all-consuming. By the time she graduated from the Juilliard School of Music in 1949, she had spent four or five years without exercising—and she had five deteriorated discs in her spine.

After surgery, Schauler was determined to overcome her disability. For the last ten years she had done calisthenics, jogged, and swum. And she has become famous for the physically demanding roles she plays. "It's a great mistake to separate the physical from the cultural," she says. "My art depends on my activity. Because I was inactive so long, I came very close to not having a career."

Barbara Yannuzzi, 1967 champion of the New York State High School Gymnastics Meet, had to give up sports entirely when she developed rheumatic fever at the age of eighteen. Four years later, as she was walking down the street, her back suddenly "gave a little slump," as she put it, "and I couldn't move." A physician told her that her stomach muscles had all but atrophied from inactivity, were no longer providing support for her spine. Now recovered from her illness, she has begun to exercise again. "My back is fine now," she says, "but it's more than that—I have much more energy and feel happier. When I was ill and couldn't do anything I had all this nervous energy building up and nowhere to put it. I was irritable and depressed all the time."

Aside from imparting energy and health, physical skill —and the good physical orientation that this imparts—acts as a preparation for and reinforcement of intellectual and creative goals. It also increases self-confidence.

"The most important thing that's happened to me over the years is that I've learned to define myself only in terms of myself," Olympic runner Francie Kraker told UPI reporter Lucinda Franks.[13]

Kraker, who began her track career because she felt like a physical misfit—taller and a faster runner than any of the boys in her Ann Arbor, Michigan, high school—now says she feels completely sure of herself. "I consider myself lucky when I see certain girls with their fleshy bodies done up in cute clothes for the benefit of their men. I feel sorry for them, because I know they don't have any idea of what it's like to get out there and move and feel the way most guys do."

Physical activity can be anything enjoyable—from gardening to mountain climbing. What's important for women is to have a positive and realistic attitude about their own strength and physical abilities, about aggressiveness, about competition. Women whose attitudes are negative in any of these four areas nearly always develop physical and/or psychological problems.

The trouble is that social attitudes make it difficult for women to feel positively about physical instincts. Guidelines for acceptable feminine behavior abound, and women who seek to develop their bodies as men do run into both prejudicial and regulatory roadblocks. Which is why—even when millions of women are getting sick of it—the femininity game is still, in the nineteen-seventies, the most acceptable female sport.

3

THE PHYSICAL BIAS

She told me it was a girl, and I turned my head away and wept. "All right," I said, "I'm glad it's a girl. And I hope she'll be a fool—that is the best thing a girl can be in this world, a beautiful little fool."

> Daisy
> *The Great Gatsby*[1]

. . . And all I could think of was how, when that certain girl played tennis, a faint moustache of perspiration appeared on her upper lip.

> Nick, the narrator
> *The Great Gatsby*[2]

I've just read *The Great Gatsby* again. Leslie Fay must have, too, because this dress makes me feel just like Scott Fitzgerald's heroine, Daisy. . . .

> Advertisement for Leslie Fay dresses
> *The New Yorker*, March 1973

As recently as the summer of 1972, taking a hike was presumed to be a risky business for the readers of *Glamour* magazine. In a June article called "You Don't Have to Be a Superwoman to Enjoy Nature," Marge Donnelly assured her readers that they could put on a backpack without jeopardizing their femininity.

"I'm hardly the lady jock type myself," she wrote. "On the slim side, with milky white skin that looks like I summer under a parasol. I hate snakes, spiders, and all the six-legged microscopic organisms. So if I can enjoy backpacking, just about anyone can."

In two sentences, Donnelly has given her readers an easy-to-follow formula for femininity: frail, pale, and entophobic—assuring them of her own impeccable credentials in the bargain. And she has implied, by juxtaposing two contradictory verbal stereotypes, that female athletes are not quite women.

This sort of thing goes on all the time in the pages of newspapers and magazines. The message is clear: "feminine" women aren't supposed to take any form of strenuous exercise seriously.

"She may wear leather as long as she cannot actually handle a motorbike," Germaine Greer has written in *The Female Eunuch*. "She may wear rubber, but it ought not to indicate that she is an expert diver or water-skier. If she wears athletic clothes, the purpose is to underline her unathleticism. She may sit astride a horse, looking soft and curvy, but she must not crouch over its neck."[3]

Calisthenics are fine—after all, they help women keep in trim for the femininity game. But the kind of exercise whose results can be measured in winning points is "unfeminine." According to traditional psychoanalytic theory, competition and aggression are masculine traits. Women who display them are suspected of sublimation and other psychological aberrations.

"Physical," where women are concerned, means "sexual," and sexual innuendo surrounds most physical activities a woman undertakes outside the boudoir. (The only women who deserve the prefix "sporting" are prostitutes.)

Sex is "recreational," men are "bedroom athletes," and a man who seduces a woman "scores."

Men's bodies are developed, women's are used. The female body is a commodity; a highly visible and salable one in the commercial world, but a handicap in the world of sport. Most women, brainwashed into playing the femininity game, eventually view themselves the way men do: as desirable objects with built-in obsolescence.

"Femininity for me (a partial listing here, for reasons of space) has meant an inordinate pride in certain dumb-luck physical prerequisites," Susan Brownmiller has written: "[A] slender body, thin wrists, modest-sized feet, a propensity for black-and-blue marks (a hallmark of delicacy?) and a happenstance of coordination which, I have been told, is rendered to the external eye as pleasing grace. Weighing in at 122, easily bruised, fine-boned and daintily thin-wristed, the world has greeted me with plus marks of approval in the social-sexual context."[4]

Brownmiller's specifications are similar to those listed in a remarkable book, *The Secret Power of Feminity* (1972):[5]

"You must drop every suggestion in speech, apparel, and manner that you are able to kill your own snakes or to take care of your own affairs or to spurn the guidance and care of man," write authors Maurine and Elbert Startup. "The air of being able to kill their own snakes is just what destroys the charm of so many teachers and competent business, careers, and professional women."

Sounding like a caricature of some Victorian ladies' handbook, the Startups seriously advise twentieth-century women to "stand before a mirror in the privacy of your room and say to yourself, 'I am just a helpless woman at the mercy of you big, strong men....'"

The different physical images of men and women and

their effects have been described by the antifeminist Dr. Esther Vilar in *The Manipulated Man*.

"It is lucky for the adult woman that men do not consider themselves beautiful," she writes, "since most men *are* beautiful. Their smooth bodies, kept trim by hard work, their strong shoulders, their muscular legs and their calibrated, meaningful movements overshadow those of women completely, even in a purely animal sense.

"And since they, unlike women, work, and their bodies are therefore preserved for continued future use, men also retain their beauty longer. As a result of their inertia, women's bodies rapidly decay and, at the age of fifty, they are nothing but indifferent heaps of human cells.

"Men are not aware of their own beauty, and no one mentions it. It would be difficult to find a description of the male body except in a medical textbook. Who would ever dream of going into great detail about the exact shape of his lips, the precise shade of his eyes. . . ."

She adds that men "seem incapable of realizing that women completely lack ambition, desire for knowledge, and the need to prove themselves."[6]

If one can manage to read Dr. Vilar dispassionately—a difficult task—one emerges with an accurate, albeit near-sighted, picture of what the femininity game has done to women. Here is a medical doctor whose contempt for her own sex infuses every paragraph. The fact that Dr. Vilar hails from Machismoland—Argentina—makes her statements only a little less horrendous. She is apparently incapable of realizing how persuasive and self-perpetuating are the physical stereotypes of femininity. Since women face punishment if they develop their bodies the way men do, few have the courage to defy social expectations. And because they do not use their bodies to compete, to develop skills, and keep in shape, they lack the self-confidence that men enjoy and quickly "go to pot" physically.

"One need only to see the importance young men place in their muscles," Simone de Beauvoir wrote in *The Second Sex*, "to understand that every subject regards his own body as his objective expression. . . . Not to have confidence in one's body is to lose confidence in oneself."[7]

But the confidence that women feel in their bodies is in direct proportion to the attraction they hold for men. Woman's physical identity is locked in the bedroom, where hair may become disheveled and feminine bodies may strain to reach orgasm and still be called beautiful. But when a female long-distance runner crosses the finish line with tangled hair and tense expression, men, and many women, are repelled.

"American society cuts the penis off the male who enters dance," says physical educator Marie Hart, "and places it on the woman who participates in competitive athletics."[8]

Only in adolescence is it acceptable for females to be physically aggressive and competitive. This attitude was unconsciously reflected in last year's television coverage of the Olympics, when ABC's commentators referred to all the women contestants as "girls." After a group of feminine activists swamped the switchboard for an hour with protests, the harried deskman finally told one caller: "You win. I just got through to Munich. They're not saying girls any more. They're calling them ladies."

There is a widespread conviction—even among many young women athletes—that continued, intensive physical training will somehow put hair on feminine chests, bulges in slim biceps, and masculine personalities in girlish heads. This belief is continually reinforced on the sports pages, where editors seem to enjoy picturing the burliest, most "masculine" female competitors and running unflattering photos of the others.

Review the sports coverage of women's events for the past year, and you'll be struck by the succession of ugly and often grotesque photos chosen to illustrate mature female athletic prowess. Anyone who saw the *New York Times* sports page for September 3, 1972, for instance, might reasonably have concluded that the three leading competitors in the Olympic Women's Pentathlon (a five-event track and field contest) were freaks. In the first of three closeup shots, attractive Marie Debourse of France was shown putting the shot with her tongue hanging out. The next frame pictured East Germany's Bruglinde Pollack in the strain of the windup, with brow furrowed and teeth bared. Finally, there was Deborah Van Kiekebelt of Canada, whose expression suggested that someone had just taken a sledge hammer to her toe.

This candid realism was spared the male track and fielders who shared the page. One was shown, hand on heart, listening to the national anthem; another was chatting amiably with an Olympic official.

With the public getting such distorted impressions from the sports page, it's not surprising that many women athletes are concerned about if not preoccupied with looking feminine.

Vicki Foltz, one of the country's best long-distance runners, told Oberlin College athletic director Jack Scott that she always worries about the size of her calf muscles. "But mostly I worry about my hair," she added. "The morning before my last big race it was hailing and blowing, but there I was in my hotel with rollers in my hair. I knew the rain would ruin my hairdo, but I fixed it anyway. I suppose it's because so many people have said women athletes look masculine, so a lot of us try, subconsciously maybe, to look as feminine as possible. . . . There are always a lot of hair ribbons in races."9

Chi Cheng, Olympic gold medalist in track and an engineering student at California State Polytech, told Scott that the main reason for her frequent public appearances was to "show off my femininity." And Donna de Varona, former swimming gold medalist, took a nationwide tour "to prove to herself and everyone else," says Buck Dawson, manager of the Swimmers' Hall of Fame, "that she's really feminine." Shortly before she made the trip, *Sports Illustrated* had run a photo of her with a caption pointing out the muscular arms on what the writer described as an "otherwise ladylike figure."

"If my daughter ever developed big leg muscles, she'd give up tennis," Chris Evert's mother said recently.

"Any woman in professional sport usually has a bad image," says Kathy Whitworth, who became the all-time big money winner in woman's golf last year when she earned $60,000 in tournament prizes (a fraction of what successful male pros get). "It's something that has haunted us for years, especially the golfers, and the problem was magnified by the man-tailored clothes we used to have to wear because nothing else was available."

A decade earlier, Iowa golfer Louise Van Horn had said, "Right now there's nothing that can be done for us golfers from the neck down, but I always make sure I wear a beautiful hat." It was 1970 before clothing manufacturers began producing good-looking styles for women golfers.

Though you'd never know it from the press coverage, the majority of female athletes have the figures, complexion, and personal vibrancy that readers of *Cosmo*, *Glamour*, et al. try to achieve with cottage cheese, Jack LaLanne, and vitamin E. For starters, there's Suzy Chaffee, a top-ranked Olympic skier and model whose picture appears more often in Dannon yogurt ads than on the sports page. Or pretty cross-country motorcyclist Terry Kleid (who got her license to race only because her first name fooled the officials). Or power-boat champion Rebecca Kapp, also a model and the first woman to complete the grueling Encenada ocean race (after stopping an hour in twenty-two-foot swells to fix a broken engine). Or jockey Robyn Smith, a former Hollywood starlet whose 20 per cent winning percentage at Aqueduct in 1972 was topped only by Angel Cordero.[10]

Indeed, women who outwardly fit the traditional stereotypes of physical beauty and femininity are overrepresented among athletes. This is no accident. It's much easier for a "pretty" girl to behave in ways that would be considered deviant in others. A girl with a muscular build and plain face will be typed as a dyke before she reaches the starting line. It takes courage to defy such a label.

Girls who are slim and curvy, on the other hand, can get away with just about anything. Evelyn Ay Sempier, Miss America of 1954, has stayed in condition for years by lifting weights. In high school and college, she was active in competitive swimming and basketball. Rita Wilson, a former Miss Tennessee, says: "I was very popular in school. When I put on track shoes it became the 'in' thing to do." She contends that many girls enter beauty contests because this is one of the few forms of competition—in the absence of athletic scholarships—where they can win college tuition money.

Then there's Gail Dearie, offensive wide receiver and defensive safety for the New York Women's Professional Football Team. Brawn and beauty? *True* magazine compared her to Raquel Welch. A mother of two, she originally got into softball "because our family didn't have too much money, so I couldn't ride or play golf or tennis. Whenever I went to a football game I'd say to myself, 'I could do that!'"

Gail Dearie found out how well she could play a few years ago during a vacation in Florida, where she came across members of the Vanderbilt University football team practicing on the beach. "I ran toward the quarterback in my bikini, clapping my hands to get him to throw the ball. He couldn't believe it, but he finally threw a long pass. When I caught it he was flabbergasted. We went on to throw the ball back and forth for about two hours, and I caught nearly everything he tossed my way, including running passes."

A regular guest on national TV talk shows, Dearie wanted to change the image of women in sports, which she calls "the most stereotyped concept of every man, woman, and child in the U.S." She adds: "There's nothing better than the feeling of using muscles."

Women like Dearie, Sempier, and Chaffee are lucky enough to have it both ways. Because of their looks, their femininity is never questioned. But it is their looks and their otherwise traditional behavior that is most often pointed out, not their athletic skill. Women athletes who are exceptionally good-looking—like Olympic gymnasts Kathy Rigby and Olga Korbut—can expect left-handed compliments in print. Though both gymnasts undoubtedly have muscles like steel springs, *Time* magazine referred to them during the Olympic Games as "tiny porcelain dolls"; Rigby was further described as the "delicate American hope." (Japanese male gymnasts were praised in the same article for their "exquisite musculature.")

There are hundreds of professional women athletes and talented amateurs who would be good fodder for feature writers. But when their stories are written up, the writers usually manage to imply that their physical activity is a curious sideline in an otherwise "normal" life.

When Nan Johnson won the national Carnegie Medal for Heroism in 1961, the Albany *Times Union* ran a photo of the heroine sitting in her living room reading a book. She had been commended for rescuing two teenage girls from drowning on the nearby Sacandaga reservoir the summer before, a feat of strength in which she had trod water—holding an unconscious girl under each arm—until help arrived.

"I told the photographer that I wanted to pose with my water skis, fishing spear, or some other sporting equipment," she says. "He gave me a choice between the kitchen sink and a book. If all I ever did was read and wash dishes, I wouldn't have had the strength to save those girls."

In the photograph, Nan Johnson was the very picture of a lady, and ladies do, of course, read books—even write them—as well as follow such cultural pursuits as painting, music, and dance. But feminine "culture" has somehow become linked with physical passivity.

The classic image of the prima donna, for instance, is one of sedentary elegance and mercurial temperament—a "lady" languishing on a chaise with a toy poodle in her lap. Most divas, in actual fact, lead extraordinarily active lives to keep in shape—but managers like Sol Hurok don't want the public to know about it.

"Mr. Hurok has instructed me never to divulge anything physical that I do because it might undermine the public image of the prima donna," says Clara Mae Turner, for years a leading singer at the New York City Opera and at the Met. "But if I wasn't physically active, I wouldn't sing well." Turner works out at gymnastics every day and walks everywhere in the city. "During the summer, at my farm in Dutchess County, I scythe grass and build stone walls. Last year I put a dam across a large stream."

Anna Moffo swims and plays tennis whenever she can, does calisthenics every morning, and thinks engaging in competitive sport is important for everyone. "For ensemble singing, it provides a background for cooperative participation. It also gives you the experience of pitting your best efforts against others. That's the only way you learn to excel at anything."

Constance Towers is a firm believer that exercise and athletics make for better performance. This star of motion pictures, soap operas and musical stage shows says, "I start and end every day with exercises. I do the Royal Canadian Air Force exercises and sometimes even use barbells. I play tennis often and swim a lot. I walk and ride a bicycle everywhere I can." She met the demands of performing nightly for an entire summer on the immense stage at Jones Beach by running a mile and a half on the beach every morning and swimming or water-skiing on the ocean or in the bay every afternoon.

The "culture" factor influences women's sports programs in high school and college. Swimming, golf, and riding are considered graceful (and, therefore, appropriately feminine). Baseball, track, and basketball are more closely competitive, sweaty, and "awkward." As Gail Dearie has noted, the "feminine" sports all require a certain amount of money to pursue—they are traditionally upper-middle- and upper-class sports. The others, while more easily accessible, bear not only a masculine but a class and cultural stigma.

"It would probably be culturally unacceptable for girls to participate in a collision sport such as football," says Fred V. Hein, Ph.D., head of the American Medical Association's

Department of Health Education. "I suspect that the great bulk of the American people would be reluctant to see girls go into weight-lifting and wrestling. At the same time, there is something very appealing about a woman in swimming, golf, or tennis. We value in this country certain attributes in men: bravery, strength, the capacity to compete in vigorous sports. But in a woman we value social graces and femininity more. These are not necessarily lost in vigorous sports, but some sports are more graceful than others."[11]

The physical bias has created more than social barriers to female athletic participation. There are national regulations prohibiting women's involvement in competitive sport, local club rules that limit women's playing hours, competitions where the prize money is thousands of dollars less. Women's collegiate athletic programs are measured in the hundreds and low thousands, while men's are in the millions. And among the thousands of coed colleges in the United States, only a handful offer even partial athletic scholarships for girls.

While making life rough for the professional woman athlete, the bias has prevented millions of other women from enjoying sport and competitive play. At some point between early adolescence and late teens, most tomboys are pressured by family and friends to give up their athletic interests. Later, those housewives who try to pursue activities they enjoyed as girls are scolded by husbands and neighbors for "not acting your age." One New York woman who enjoys jogging around her neighborhood before dinner says she finally started taking her dog along to avoid being kidded. "Now when people ask me what on earth I'm doing, I say I'm running him."

Resentment of athletic women tends to increase in proportion to their accomplishments. Women pros in every field have run the gantlet of derision and discrimination.

"Men don't treat women as equals on skis or anywhere else," says Olympian Suzy Chaffee. "We're sex objects there, too." As an example, she cites something called the K-2 Plus Shirt Contest, held every Olympic season in off-hours. Team members are chosen on the basis of who looks best in a T-shirt, says Chaffee, "and the winner is the one who takes off her shirt before she gets to the end of the run. And that's the kind of cubbyhole men want to keep us in."

Penny Pitou, U.S. Olympic ski champ in 1960, believes the physical bias is as prevalent among women as among men.

"A woman once wrote me a fan letter saying what a wonderful young woman she thought I was. She said she hoped my daughter would grow up to be just like me and then added, 'please don't let the little girl ski.' That's the kind of thing I've always had to face. People try to mind my business, to turn me into something I'm not. When I'm in public, I'm conscious of everyone sizing up my clothes and my behavior—usually with some surprise. I guess women expect a ski champ to come to a party in a man's suit or in blue jeans. They also expect you to be dumb—maybe because a lot of male pros are—yet the athletic women I've known have all been intellectually outstanding. Someday I'm going to build a fence around my hundred and fifty acres and do what I damn please."

Until recently, the women's liberation movement has had little to say about sexism in sport. In July 1972 the National Organization for Women established a committee on women's sports, and has since sponsored one major workshop on sport. Most of the work, however, is currently being done by individual women athletes. Possibly this is because many women consciously or unconsciously share male attitudes about women in sport, viewing athletics not only as an exclusively male province—which it is, by default—but also as a relatively unimportant issue—which it is not.

It is hoped that physical equality will eventually be seen by women as a basic right, not extraneous to feminism but intrinsic to it. The concept may not seem as relevant, perhaps, as a ballot or a paycheck. But a woman is a girl through many years when the goals of liberation are not immediately relevant to her. And the physical bias has warped the personalities of millions of women long before they were old enough to care about politics or a career.

4

THE FEMININE PHYSIQUE

> So far as the excellence of a performance depends
> mainly on the kind of muscles, bones, size, and
> strength that one has, women can be dealt with as
> fractional men.
>
> Paul Weiss
> *Sport: A Philosophic Inquiry*[1]

Feminine strength and endurance have always been
economic assets for men—a source of cheap labor for business
and industry, of unpaid labor in the home. For centuries,
women have toiled on farms and in factories. Crawling on
their hands and knees, stripped to the waist, they have pulled
loads through coal mine tunnels too narrow to accommodate
a horse. In Russia today, women build roads, lay bricks,
and operate heavy equipment. Back in our own frontier days,
every pioneer woman had to be able to do "a man's work."

But not long after paychecks entered the picture, the
feminine physique became a liability. It was all right for
women and girls to strain their backs and their eyes at looms
and sewing machines twelve hours a day, seven days a week.
Yet when the typewriter was invented, promising women
better wages and working conditions, their capacity to stand

the physical strain of operating such machines was questioned. As a result, until World War I, most secretaries were male.

Today, most people—certainly most men—invoke physical differences between the sexes as evidence of insurmountable barriers to athletic equality. Because of these differences, women are said to be more suited to some sports than others—and unfit to compete directly with men in *any* contact sport.

"One way of dealing with these disparities between the athletic promise and achievements of men and women," says Yale philosophy professor Paul Weiss, "is to view women as truncated males. As such they should be permitted to engage in such sports as men do (except where these still invite unusual dangers for them), but in foreshortened versions."

Aristotle referred to women as "misbegotten men"; Freud called them "castrated." Now Weiss comes up with "truncated men" who must be "permitted" to engage in sports.

If a man can enlist in the armed forces knowing he may not survive his tour of duty, it seems reasonable that a woman be allowed to decide whether she wants to risk losing a tooth or bruising a breast in athletic competition.

Professor Weiss, who, as the author of *Sport: A Philosophical Inquiry,* has quite a following among physical educators, disagrees. "It is part of our cultural heritage to make an effort to avoid having women maimed, disfigured, or hurt," he writes. "That is one reason why they do not usually engage in and are not physically allowed to compete in such contact sports as boxing, wrestling, football, and rugby, with inexplicable exceptions being made for karate and lacrosse."[2]

Ever since men assumed control of women's sports in the early nineteen-twenties, most physical educators have shared Weiss's views, bolstering their arguments with questionable facts about female physiognomy. These "facts" are worth reviewing, if only because so many women have been brainwashed into believing them.

The National Little League, for instance, bars girls from playing ball on the grounds that they have slower reaction times, less muscle fiber, and weaker bones.

As far as reaction time is concerned, the Little League's conclusions were drawn from a study of nine hundred women of all ages who were compared to men in similar age brackets. No attempt was made to carry out a controlled study of men and women with similar athletic backgrounds. Most boys play football and baseball throughout childhood. How many girls do?

As for muscle mass, women do indeed, according to some studies, have roughly half the muscle mass of men. And men are, on the average, a third stronger than women. But as far back as 1918, the *Journal of the American Medical Association* attributed much of this disparity to male muscle-flexing.[3] Most women are in poor physical condition, sedentary, and often overweight. Were they given the opportunities men have to keep fit, the strength gap would narrow considerably.

Obviously, few women, even if they cared to, could attain the proportions of the six-foot-four, 290-pound defensive end drafted a couple of years ago by one pro football team. But size and strength aren't always indicative of physical power. In golf, for example, it's assumed that women, being smaller, can't drive the ball as far as a man. Some golf courses, like the one in Darien, Connecticut, even specify on their tournament programs that certain greens require fewer shots for men than for women. Men are expected to reach the four-hundred-yard fifth green in Darien in two shots; women in three. Well, Laura Baugh, who stands five two and weighs

110 pounds, made the fifth green at Darien in two strokes at the age of fifteen.

The petite build of many top women gymnasts belies their extraordinary strength. Muriel Davis Grossfeld, the 1960 U.S. Olympic gymnast, is just over five feet tall. Yet fitness tests at the University of Illinois revealed that she was as strong as the average male college athlete.

A few years ago, U.S. women's water ski champion Dicksie Ann Hoyt's slalom score was higher than any of the male competitors'. How had she done it? asked one of them. "Brute strength," said Dicksie. On an earlier occasion she'd taken on a string of linemen from the University of Florida football team in arm-wrestling and beat all but one. ("He was a skinny guy," she said later, "but he was real strong.")

So strength is relative, often deceptive, and frequently irrelevant in comparison to skill. But what about bones? It's true, as the Little League contends, that women's bones ossify sooner than men's. That's because girls reach puberty earlier. But this is a plus, not a minus. Adolescent boys run a greater risk of injury because their bones aren't fully ossified until their late teens. At the 1972 conference on women in sport at Penn State University, it was reported that girls and women have fewer orthopedic injuries than men—partly because of earlier ossification, partly because, at maturity, women's bones are harder than men's.

Other so-called disadvantages women have to put up with are smaller hearts, higher pulse rates, smaller lung capacity, lower aggressive instincts, bad spatial orientation, and more body fat—all of which supposedly combine to give them less endurance.

First of all, taking on this impressive list in order, women's smaller hearts can work relatively harder than men's without any ill effects. At the Penn State conference, medical researchers reported that a pulse of 200 could be attained without risk in a fifteen-year-old girl, while adult women athletes can reach 180 easily during exertion—about 20 beats faster than a man.

Going on to the lungs, we find that the average adult male has a 30 per cent greater "aerobic capacity" or "vital capacity" (the volume of air that can be exhaled from the lungs after breathing in deeply) than the average woman. This is partly because men, being bigger, have bigger lungs; partly because the statistics are stacked in favor of men. There have been no large-scale studies done on female respiration. Until there are, this difference must remain theoretical.[4]

As for aggression, men apparently do have a natural edge here. Studies of infant male primates and little boys indicate that males play rougher and show a greater preference for bruising physical contact than do female apes and little girls. On the other hand, little boys are encouraged from infancy to be aggressive and little girls are punished for displays of aggressiveness; so it's hard to know where to draw the line. An authority on aggression, Dr. John Scott, of the Bowling Green University Research Center, has demonstrated that both girls and boys have an aggressive drive; he feels the difference is merely one of degree.[5]

Any innate difference in aggressiveness is generally agreed to be hormonal. Androgen and estrogen, the male and female hormones that produce secondary sexual characteristics, have a profound influence on the physical appearance and the temperament of both men and women. Androgen, the male hormone, has been shown in rats to strike some chemical chord that increases aggressive behavior. Hormones also influence the size of bones and the character of the muscular system. Estrogen, the female hormone, inhibits muscle and bone growth; androgen encourages it.

Yet among members of each sex, a good deal of variation occurs in the amount of hormonal output—and, even, in the chemical concentration of the hormones. Women who secrete greater amounts of androgen are usually more aggressive than others. They also tend to have better-developed muscles and bigger bones.

Sex differences begin to show up in the fetus five to six weeks after conception, when the male embryo is given an "androgen bath." Until then the human embryo is essentially female. The male XY chromosome, the genetic unit that determines sex, is really an incomplete female XX chromosome with the leg of one X broken off. Because his smaller chromosome can't carry all the duplicate genetic information contained on the female unit, the male is more prone to hereditary disease. In a woman, defects on one gene can be corrected by automatic substitution of healthy components from the twin gene; but in men, many of these genetic alternatives are missing. (Aristotle, Freud, and Weiss, take note! If either sex deserves to be called "misbegotten," "castrated," or "truncated," it is the male, with his fractured sex chromosome.)

Chromosomes have recently become something of an international issue with the discovery of hermaphroditism at the Olympics. (Occasionally a biological short circuit occurs during fetal development, resulting in a hermaphrodite—a person who either possesses the sexual characteristics of one sex and the chromosomal pattern of the other, or who exhibits primary and secondary sexual characteristics of both sexes.) The few hermaphrodites who have turned up at the Olympics have gotten more than their share of publicity, and the public image of the female Olympic athlete is, as a result, that of a big, square-shouldered track and field star. Before being allowed to compete, all female Olympic athletes now must have their chromosomes analyzed—not in the privacy of a physician's office, but in a line up, with the male-or-female verdict rendered as each participant reaches the end of the queue. Until 1971, cells were collected from the inside of the athletes' cheeks and examined under a microscope. Today, strands of hair are tested instead; but women who have stood in the line up still describe the experience humiliating.

The chromosome tests have served to cast suspicion on the sexual identity of all ruggedly built women. Our current feminine body ideal is the thin, delicate build characteristic of most fashion models. In the past, the feminine body ideal was often pear-shaped—certainly heavier and more rounded than the ultrathinness for which many women now starve. The muscular build typical of most men has never been the Western world's ideal for women. Muscular women have, in fact, been consistently discriminated against as unfeminine.

The burly woman athlete image has persuaded a lot of women that strenuous athletic activity leads to ungainly muscles. It isn't so. "Proper training is the answer," says Walter Kostric, trainer of Canadian track and field star Debbie Van Kiekebelt. "Some exercises can develop protruding muscles, but others don't. A good coach knows the difference."

"Contrary to lay opinion," exercise physiologists Carl E. Klafs and Daniel Druheim have written in *Psychology Today*, [6] "participation in sports does not masculinize women or build excess muscle." They added that women with muscular builds are often successful as athletes, but that athletics doesn't create heavy muscles.

61

Most women have more body fat than men. And where fat exists, muscle obviously doesn't. Conditioning has a lot to do with this, of course, but even physically active women do have more fat than men. In some areas of athletics—endurance swimming, for instance—a little extra fat can be an advantage, providing warmth and buoyancy. But when a woman is in top form, the extra fat doesn't affect her performance at all, in *any* sport.

Another much-touted difference between the sexes is spatial orientation. Men are supposedly better at orienting themselves in space—at "keeping their eye on the ball," using their own physical positions as a reference point to activity around them.

Women tend to use peripheral objects as points of reference and are easily distracted by visual stimuli. Men, for instance, can pick a figure out of a complex pattern more readily than women. Perhaps, it has been suggested, this is a throwback to prehistoric times when life depended on a man's ability to keep his eye on a fleeting stag in the underbrush. More likely, it's a psychological difference, resulting from greater self-confidence on the part of men.

Joan Strati, physical education director at the Mamaroneck School in Mamaroneck, New York, found that girl athletes consistently underestimated their own physical measurements. Asked to guess the length of their arm span, for instance, thirty girls estimated the distance to be less than it actually was. A control group of nonathletes yielded identical answers—confirming the finding that women generally have an inferior body image, reflecting lack of self-confidence. They rely on their environment rather than themselves as reference points, and are consequently distracted by extrapersonal influences.[7]

Dr. Julia Sherman, associate scientist at the University

of Wisconsin Psychiatric Institute, reported the preliminary results of a study on sex differences in spatial orientation. It was her hypothesis that education, especially in elementary and high schools, short-changes females by concentrating more on verbal than on spatial training. Although it has been believed for years that spatial ability could *not* be enhanced by training, Dr. Sherman found definite improvement of this ability in girls given special visual training before testing.[8]

Until now, this discussion of the feminine physique has been limited to Western culture. But in other parts of the world women are physically equal or superior to men. Robert Briffault has noted, for example, that among the Bushmen, women are an average of four centimeters taller than the men; and that Arab, Afghanistan, and Druse women are as tall as their men and as strongly developed. "Among the Adombies of the Congo, the women are often stronger than the men and more finely developed," he writes. "And among the Ashira, the men are not nearly so finely built as the women. A Kikuyu man is quite unequal to carrying a load that his women think nothing of. . . . A crew of Dayak women can beat a crew of Malay men."

Though many anthropologists have cited the prehistoric role of man as hunter to explain his athletic superiority today, Briffault (and, more recently, Yale's David Philbeam) contends that the primitive division of labor is not based on female physical inferiority.

"There are numerous reports of women hunters among uncultured peoples," says Briffault. "In West Africa the women formerly used to carry bows and arrows and go out hunting without the aid of men. Among the Hill Dayaks of Borneo, a spear is part of the equipment of every woman, and they go hunting with dogs. Of the women of Nicaragua, we are told that they could run and swim and shoot with bows and arrows as well as the men. . . ."[9]

It seems clear from these examples that differences in reaction time, muscle mass, bones, hearts, lungs, hormones, strength, spatial orientation, and body fat—when they exist —don't necessarily make much of a difference where relative performance is concerned. But what about menstruation, pregnancy, and endurance? Here, surely, are three clear-cut examples of inferiority.

Female students are still getting excused from gym classes at "that time of the month," it's often argued. How can a woman athlete compete on the same level with men if she's likely to be out of commission three days out of thirty?

Because she's not. At the 1964 Olympics in Melbourne, for example, six gold medal winners were menstruating at the time of their victories. A Hungarian physician, Dr. Gyula J. Erdelyi, has found that it is largely psychological rather than physical factors that effect performance during menstruation. One third of Erdelyi's study group of 729 women athletes showed *no* change in performance during menstruation, a third declined, and a third improved.[10]

Many women athletes believe that strenuous physical activity eliminates menstrual difficulties. Track and field star Debbie Van Kiekebelt says that menstruation improves her performance; in fact, two of her Canadian national championships were won on first days of menstrual periods. "For a woman in good condition, the period is a natural and emotionally rewarding release," says her coach, Walter Kostric.

"Most of women's fears about exercise and menstruation are unfounded," says Dr. Clayton Thomas, a member of the U.S. Olympic Team's medical staff and medical research director for Tampax. "Women athletes have much less difficulty in this area than those who are sedentary."

Drs. Franz Alexander and Boris B. Rubenstein concluded

after extensive study that the production of estrogen during menstruation "stimulates the ego to higher integration and coordination."[11] And Dr. Ferguson Anderson of Glasgow University has only good news about hormonal effects on feminine endurance. "Women live longer than men because nature has equipped them with a six-cylinder engine compared with man's four-cylinder one," he says. "Women have a better heart and better system generally."[12]

Recently Dr. Grace Fischer, of the University of Pennsylvania, stated that women probably have fewer heart attacks than men because estrogen keeps their arteries more elastic, helping to offset arterial sclerosis and fat buildup.[13]

All the myths and distortions about hormones in general and menstruation in particular may be a carryover from the very ancient past. In *The First Sex,* Elizabeth Gould Davis notes that the old matriarchial calendar was based on the twenty-eight-day lunar and menstrual cycle—a thirteen-month calendar. Ever since the patriarchal takeover (circa 1000 B.C.), menstruation and the number 13 have been taboo.[14]

As for pregnancy, here's another interesting statistic: ten of the twenty-six Soviet women champions at the Melbourne Olympics were pregnant at the time of their victories.

Contrary to popular belief and some medical opinion, there is plenty of evidence that pregnancy *enhances* physical performance during the first six months, and that exercise is seldom harmful to either the mother or the fetus. Two thirds of the 729 athletes interviewed by Dr. Erdelyi said they continued their sports during the first three months of pregnancy. And efficiency tests on another group of 33 pregnant women showed that during the twenty-fourth to thirty-third week after conception they were more efficient than their nonpregnant counterparts.

Still another study revealed that 70 per cent of a group

of 207 women athletes continued their sports through the sixth month of pregnancy. One rower, who competed when three months pregnant, came in first in a field of 17 nonpregnant rivals. A discus thrower who was four and a half months pregnant won a national championship at the Compeorata de Athletismo de Europa.[15]

Dr. Erdelyi has concluded that pregnancy and sport are not only compatible but desirable, leading to easier labor and early resumption of normal activities after giving birth. Deliveries among female athletes, he found, were 87 per cent faster than among nonathletes; and the time athletes spent in the second stage of labor was half the norm. The figures were the same for top athletes and mediocre ones, which would suggest that general physical conditioning rather than prowess is the determinant.

All in all, it is far more natural for a woman to be active than sedentary during pregnancy. Years ago, when pregnancy was treated as an illness and women were "confined," the risk of complications during delivery was strikingly higher than it is now. Circulation, vital to the health of the child, and muscle tone, which speeds delivery, are improved by physical activity.

Bad falls are obviously to be avoided during pregnancy, but the female reproductive system is designed to protect the fetus against all but the most severe accidents. The uterus is surrounded by structures of almost the same specific gravity as itself, with no air space around it. It floats in a pool of pelvic viscera, much as an egg floats in a tightly sealed jar of water. When shaken, it simply can't fly violently through the fluid. (If you want to test this out, place a raw egg in an airtight jar full of water. No amount of shaking that doesn't smash the jar will injure the egg.)

When it comes to endurance, men, because of their greater

strength and lung capacity, supposedly become exhausted less quickly than women. "Look at all the male long-distance runners that women haven't begun to catch up to," we're often told. But there are many more men than women running marathons, and in the Olympics women aren't allowed to run more than 1500 meters, so this evidence is only relative. Furthermore, women have greater *tolerance* for fatigue, which tends to even things out.

And let us not forget Diane Struble Rippon, a woman who in 1958 swam forty-two miles in New York's Lake George. Jack Dempsey had proposed the challenge in 1928, and the best swimmers in the world had tried—and failed—to meet it. Though greater distances have been conquered in other bodies of water, Lake George's turbulence and icy temperatures demand almost superhuman endurance.

Rippon, who was pushing thirty at the time and in a condition which she described as a "physical and emotional wreck," decided to get back in shape by taking on Lake George. After a few months of training and careful preparation, she dived in. Toward the evening of her second day in the water, Diane stepped ashore at the southern tip of Lake George. "I wish the lake had been longer," she said. "I could have gone further."

A few years later a U.S. Marine set out to duplicate her feat—"to uphold manly valor." He did make it (in two and a half days), becoming the second person and first man to swim Lake George. But rumor has it that he was out of commission for several days afterward. Diane was feeling pretty normal, she said, ten minutes after drying off.

For an encore, Rippon swam around Manhattan Island, navigating both the East River and the Hudson, taking into account ocean tides to calculate the precise moment she would arrive at each location. Just off the Seventy-ninth

Street boat basin, she had to tread water for three hours while the New York police checked out her credentials, then refused to let her go around again.

After that she crossed Boston Harbor with ease and later swam thirty-six miles in Lake Champlain. By this time she had built up quite a following, and scores of boats gathered to escort her across. A few hours out a storm came up, and all boats except the pilot boat streaked for cover. Her husband and three other men in the pilot boat tried to persuade her to turn back with them; she refused, then completed the crossing. When a reporter asked Rippon what was on her mind while she was on the lake in the middle of the night with a storm raging around her, she said, "I worried about what I'd do if that boat overturned and I had to save all those men."

In 1963, at age thirty-five, Rippon entered the sixty-mile Lake Michigan swim "just for fun. I only went thirty miles," she said. "My new baby was a few months old, and I couldn't risk being out of commission with five kids to dress and feed."

That particular contest was won by the thirty-four-year-old Egyptian Abdel Latif Abo Heif, who swam the sixty miles from Chicago, Illinois, to Benton Harbor, Michigan, in thirty-four hours and forty-five minutes, never going slower than sixty strokes per minute.

For the first fifteen hours, Latif was paced by Gretta Anderson at seventy-two strokes a minute. But a $15,000 winner-take-all prize was at stake, and Latif really poured it on ("I had to get that woman out of my wake," he told reporters). He broke Anderson's pace and went on to an incredible victory.

Diane Rippon was one of the first to congratulate Latif. Later she told a friend, "I didn't mind being out of the contest.

It was a great experience just to be in the same water with such a remarkable athlete."

Most men are not as gracious when they lose to women. Nor are they at all eager to reexamine misconceptions about the feminine physique in light of all the new evidence. Dr. Eleanor Maccoby of Stanford University, a psychologist who has done extensive research on sex differentiation and has questioned for years the relevance of physical differences to women's participation in competitive sport, is not taken seriously by many of her colleagues. "In our circle we treat her with amusement," says the head of the Yale Physiology and Anatomy Department. "It's a well-known biological fact that the male is twice as strong as the female."

Ho hum. And more yawns for Paul Weiss, who not only persists with his reactionary notions about physique but extends them to include athletic prowess as well. "Women are unable to compete successfully with the best of men," he says, "except in sports which emphasize accuracy, skill, or grace—shooting, fancy skating, diving, and the like. Their bones, contours, musculature, growth rate, size, proportion, and reaction times do not allow them to do as well as men in sports which put a premium on strength and speed."[16]

That red flag is worth exploring further.

5

GAMES WOMEN CAN'T PLAY

There are, of course, one or two noteworthy exceptions to this rule of male superiority, but they're
so exceptional that they shouldn't inspire you to
dream of someday endorsing cereals. . . .
                                    Ralph Schoenstein
                                    Seventeen
                                    June 1971

Once upon a spring day in Haverill, Massachusetts, a twelve-
year-old redhead named Sharon Poole made a brief, two-
game debut as centerfielder for the Little League Rotary
Indians. As she shagged balls expertly and knocked in a
decisive run, the parents of her teammates booed her from
the stands. Afterward, the local League manager kicked Sharon off the team, fired her coach, and erased the official
records of the two games she played in.

"Girls shouldn't play baseball," snapped one mother. "It
isn't ladylike."

The national officers of the Little League were more cir-
cumspect. "The evidence available to us right now shows
that it would be wrong to subject girls to possible injury,"
said Dr. Creighton Hale, research director and executive vice-

president of the NLL. "We believe they should play in non-contact sports like golf and swimming—not baseball, football, or rugby."[1]

The editorial page of the *Boston Globe* struck home: "Obviously a parent will lose his or her sense of self-esteem if a girl strikes out his or her son or hits a homer off him or throws him out at second."

Clearly, the basic issue was not intellectual but emotional. When a wcnan beats a man on the playing field, her reward is more likely to be anger than applause. Woman's traditional role in sports, as elsewhere, continues to be supportive, not competitive. The female majority is expected to stay on the sidelines, either cheering the team on, providing musical or acrobatic diversion at halftime, or feeding their escorts box lunches.

Apart from the questionable biological evidence and scholarly arguments previously mentioned, which are invoked to keep women out of competitive sport, the male-dominated sports world has made certain assumptions about women—based largely on fantasy—and then arranged matters so that women would continue to conform to these assumptions.

Times haven't changed as much as the relatively extensive television coverage of women's Olympic events might suggest. The view from Munich was spectacular but illusory. Olympic competitors represent only a handful of talented women athletes—and most of them have suffered for their competence. For the rest, physical and competitive emancipation are a long way off.

The few women who have the opportunity to turn pro have a rough time. Prize money, for instance, is minuscule in comparison to men's. One golfer estimated that the combined total of all women's tournament purses is less than a single purse in a male tournament. While top men pros earn annual incomes in the hundreds of thousands, Kathy Whitworth became the all-time money winner in women's gold last year, with winnings of $60,000.

Women pros also have to put up with biased male judges, referees, and other men in positions of authority.

"Women are pushed around in golf—on both an amateur and professional level," says Maureen Orcutt, ten-time winner of the women's Metropolitan Golf Tournament and the former golf columnist for the *New York Times*. Last year, she says, the MGT was held—at the insistence of the male pro in charge—during the height of Hurricane Agnes.

"It was Tuesday, raining buckets, with a terrible wind and branches falling all around us," she says, "but he decided that the course was playable. When we suggested postponement, the pro gave us a little lecture and said that 'every round of golf is a good test of playing skill.' At one point he called a twenty-minute break and we all stood there in the downpour. The next day, when the rain stopped for a while and the course was really playable, the pro called the PGA commissioner and asked him to call off the tournament. The men got us both ways."

On most private courses there are rules limiting playing hours for women to certain days or hours. At Maureen Orcutt's own club—the White Beeches in Haworth, New Jersey—women aren't allowed on the links until after 1 P.M. At the Ridgewood, New Jersey, club, it's 2 P.M. Many other clubs limit women's play to the daylight hours, cutting out the working girl. Such restrictions are about as liberated as the athletic policies in Baghdad: women there may swim in the Tigris for four hours a day; men have its use for the other twenty.

Lack of golfing opportunity isn't limited to the United

States. In 1968, a fan who had read that British women golf pros were on tour in America went to watch them. "I see only three of you could make it," he said. "*All* three of us," replied one of the women. "English men really don't like women to play golf. We have nowhere and no one to play as pros."

The U.S. Olympic Committee has different rules and regulations for men and women, a policy that Olga Connally disparaged in a *New York Times* interview. "They treat us like sheep," the thirty-six-year-old record-holder for the women's discus told a reporter a month before the Olympics. "Everything for the men is optional. They don't have to go to the training camp in Eugene, they don't have to go to the camp in Maine, they don't have to go to the August meet in Oslo. If they want to pass up everything, they can simply report to Washington on August 18 and leave for Munich."[2]

Connally, who was recovering from the flu when asked to report for training, requested that she be allowed to bypass the meets. She was turned down and had to appeal to a special games preparation committee for sick leave.

"My obligation, if anything, is to my children, community, and myself," she said. "I don't have any respect for the Olympics Committee because they haven't earned it."

During the 1968 Olympics a woman contestant was expelled for what officials termed "misconduct involving a member of the opposite sex"—a member of the men's track team. He was allowed to stay. She had to go home.

On the racetrack, the bias against female jockeys makes it difficult for them to get mounts. Robyn Smith, who won her first race in 1969, was able to get only sixty-seven mounts during the following year. Bobby Woodhouse, who won his first race about the same time as she did, got 1657 mounts in that year.

The illusion of athletic equality is kept alive by men like Ralph Schoenstein, who said in his *Seventeen* article, "Can You Really Go Play with the Boys?," "No matter what sport you select, at least you have the comfort of knowing that it's no longer socially unacceptable for a girl to defeat a boy. . . . Yes, it's no longer unacceptable—it's just very hard if he's more than ten."

First of all, beating a man is still not socially acceptable. But the main message Schoenstein is passing on to his teen-age readers in this article is that no matter how hard a girl tries, no matter how good she gets, she'll never be able to catch up to a man. So why try?

Earlier in the piece, Schoenstein quotes tennis player Billie Jean King as saying, "I don't think girls should play against men. They should stay in their own league."

It sounds as though King sees no value at all in mixed competition. In fact, she perfected her own game by playing and beating dozens of men. A more thorough interview would have disclosed that one of the reasons she no longer wants to do so is that so many men are lousy sports. "Men just don't like women's tennis," she said a few months after talking to Schoenstein. "They don't respect us and they're jealous of our success. It's an ego thing. They simply don't want us to succeed. You'll find a lot of animosity between top-ranking men and women players."

"Women play about 25 per cent as good as men, so they should get about 25 per cent of the money men receive," Bobby Riggs was quoted in a *Time* article (May 14, 1973) before his match with Margaret Smith Court.

Court, as the world knows, was soundly beaten by Riggs, who promoted the match as a man-vs.-women's-lib showdown. But women tennis players have admitted for years that any of the top twenty (some say forty) men could easily beat the best woman player—a considerably smaller percentage than Riggs allowed. Since Riggs is one of best male players in the history of tennis, and since Court has a reputation for being psychologically vulnerable, the outcome was not surprising.

In any case, if men are really as sure of their superior ability as men like Riggs and Schoenstein assert, what's all the fuss about? Why can't Sharon Poole or eleven-year-old Maria Pepe of Hoboken (also out in left field now) stay in the Little League? After all, they tried out for the team and were as good as at least half of the boys. Was Sharon booed because the parents were concerned about her supposedly slower reaction time or because her bones will ossify sooner?

It seems more likely that because Poole and Pepe were challenging the myth of masculine superiority, the *parents* felt threatened. Certainly it's true that in some sports greater masculine strength will give the best man an edge over the best woman. But the fact that the average man is bigger and stronger than the average woman has been wrongly interpreted not as a dimensional disparity but as a general proof of superiority in acts of physical skill. Bigger is supposed to equal better.

"In almost every sport, one of the keys to championship is simply strength," says Schoenstein. He then goes on to quote Al Silverman, editor of *Sport* magazine: "It's all a matter of muscularity. Women have a chance to beat men only in a sport that calls for far more grace than strength—figure skating, for instance. Even as jockeys women can't be as good as a man because strength is still needed to whip and control the horse."[3]

Then why is jockey Robyn Smith so often in the winner's

circle at New York's Aqueduct racetrack? Why is tiny Kathy Kusner one of the world's top riders? And how did Princess Anne manage to walk off with most of the blue ribbons in a mixed competition in England a few years ago?

Anyone who knows horses can tell you that a rider controls a mount through balance, legs, and hands. Unless he knew how to ride, the burliest fullback in the world couldn't control a 1500-pound thoroughbred who had different ideas—though it might be fun to see him try.

But the whole strength argument is really beside the point.

"In sport the end in view is . . . the attainment of perfection within the limitations of each physical type," wrote Simone de Beauvoir in *The Second Sex*. "The featherweight boxing champion is as much a champion as the heavyweight."

Yet there are few competent women drivers who haven't been told they *don't* drive "like a woman." And athletic girls are used to hearing that they don't run or throw like women—when, in fact, they're simply displaying skill in a nonsexual act of physical coordination.

Women are regularly judged against male yardsticks. On the rare occasion when a man does compliment a woman for superior athletic performance, he usually ends up comparing her to himself. Jack Scott, director of physical education at Oberlin College, recalls the praise showered on gold medal diver Micki King by her coach: "He said she was going to be great because she 'dives like a man.' My immediate reaction was that she sure as hell doesn't dive like me or any other man I ever met. In fact she doesn't dive like 99 per cent of the men in America. What she does do is dive *correctly*."[4]

"Little boys throw like most big girls do," says Judy Mage. "I'm not a natural athlete—small, skinny, not particularly strong or well coordinated. But I trained myself to throw and catch well by practicing every day from the age of eight to fourteen. By the time I quit at fourteen—to become a lady—I was really good. Most girls can't run, throw, or hit well because they haven't been as lucky as I was. They had had no opportunity to learn."

Three years ago, divorced, in her early thirties, and living on the Lower East Side of New York, Mage decided to take up baseball again. "It was early spring, and I wanted to get out and throw a ball. I used to bike out along the river looking for a game, then hang around trying to get into it. I found that I was most acceptable to teenage Puerto Rican boys. Even at my age my skills had improved, and I was better than I had been twenty years before."

Unless women have a chance to match talents against their equals, regardless of sex, they'll never get to be the best at anything. And there will never be a true picture of feminine athletic ability until women have the same opportunities and motivation to compete that men have. Right now they are psychologically discouraged from competition. And the opportunities simply aren't there.

The first barrier is parents—and what social scientists call "achievement models." Unless she's lucky enough to have a mother or aunt who has defied the stereotypes (or a very liberal father), a young woman doesn't have many examples to follow. And in the sports world, success models are even rarer.

Girls who didn't tune into the 1972 Olympics may have to wait another four years to see an attractive woman athlete. The press coverage is distorted, and in books, comics, movies, and on television female athletes, or any physically competent women, are virtually nonexistent—except when they appear as dingbats or villains. (In a recent episode of

Mod Squad, a girl gymnast working out on a trampoline turned out to be keeping fit for a life of collegiate crime. She eventually gets locked up by one of the Mod Squad, who first demonstrates that he can outflip and outtwist her.)

Except for the television heroines of the British series *The Avengers* and *The Champions,* leading ladies on the screen or in print usually toe the feminine line.

Nancy Drew, the girl detective whose exploits have influenced generations of teenage mystery fans is, despite her ingenuity, basically sweet, pretty, and nonaggressive. Though Nancy does play golf and have adventures, her boy friend Ned Nickerson is continually demonstrating his physical and intellectual superiority by getting her out of jams.

Lois Lane, girl reporter, usually got into trouble when she pursued a story too aggressively; Superman had to fly in and bail her out. And the comic-book exploits of Captain Marvel were always far beyond those of his sister Mary. "She was no Wonder Woman," recalls a former Captain Marvel fan. "Mary Marvel was a drip."

Today's textbooks follow the same pattern. The first national conference on sexual stereotypes, in 1972 (sponsored by the National Education Association and the U.S. Office of Education), reported that the textbooks used in spelling, reading, math, science, and social studies depicted boys as strong, intelligent, adventurous, independent, and courageous. Girls were shown doing housework, playing with dolls, or watching boys do something.

With Cinderella and Sleeping Beauty still setting the pace, it's not surprising to find most women back at the starting gate. Those who do go out for competitive sport usually have older brothers who serve as behavior models. Girls with this background, says physical educator Eileen Portz of Penn State University, are overrepresented among athletes and physical education majors. But firstborn girls whose parents fit the masculine-feminine stereotypes are less inclined to go out for sports; they tend to follow their parents' example.[5]

The same pattern holds for boys, but with predictably different results. Studies of firstborn boys who imitate their fathers have shown that the majority are high achievers who excel in all the typically male pursuits. When the space program began, for example, all but one of the astronauts on the early Apollo flights were only or firstborn children.

If a girl is lucky enough to have an older brother or supportive parents and is able to buck the social pressures against competing, she may reach high school and find there's nowhere to play.

Terry Wood, the daughter of a golf pro and a 1972 graduate of an Atlanta, Georgia, high school who has hit 290 yards with a good tail wind and frequently scores in the low seventies, says, "At my high school they had a rule. The golf team could consist of eight *male* members. If it hadn't been for that one word, I'd have been number one on the team."

High school sports facilities for girls are usually either inadequate or nonexistent, while the boys' facilities are inaccessible. Two regulations from New Jersey are typical:

"No girl may be permitted to participate in an interscholastic athletic contest with boys." That's rule Z of the Girls' Interscholastic Regulations.

"A female pupil may not be a member of a boys' secondary athletic team in team sports or in individual sports against male representatives." That's the boys' interscholastic regulation.

Linda Ruppert, top-ranked by the U.S. Lawn Tennis Association, has been unable to get on the men's team at

Liberty High School in Bethlehem, Pennsylvania; and in Teaneck, New Jersey, talented Abbe Seldin was forced to sit the tennis season out because of the restrictive laws. "I've seen Abbe play in a couple of women's tournaments and she's good," head Teaneck coach Art Christensen told the *Philadelphia Inquirer*. "But playing against girls, she'll only meet two or three good opponents a year. If you want to be tops, you need more than that."

Meanwhile, the New Jersey Interscholastic Athletic Association has ruled that girls may play with boys on their school teams. However, Seldin's local coach, Christensen, has moved, and his replacement declares he will do anything to prevent girls from playing on the same teams as boys.

Women like Seldin and Ruppert must have been disheartened by a 1972 State Supreme Court decision against Renee Gregario of Asbury Park, New Jersey. Miss Gregario, a runnerup in the State Lawn Tennis Association Tournament, had tried to get on the men's team at her high school as an entree to a later athletic scholarship—her only hope of a college education after her father's death. The court turned her down, insisting on a full jury trial at some distant future date.

Those women who do succeed in getting on men's teams face the bias of outside coaches. Last year, despite a new ruling by the California Community College Association permitting coeducational competition, players for San Diego City College walked off the basketball court when a woman substitute was sent in by the opposition. With less than four minutes left in the game, San Bernardino coach Ray Blake sent in eighteen-year-old Sue Palmer, whereupon San Diego forfeited the game.

In 1963, though tennis star Roberta Allison at the University of Alabama had won twenty matches against men during her sophomore year, the University of Illinois team refused to compete with Alabama if she appeared on the courts. Roberta sat the game out, and her team lost. Mississippi's coach, Tom Sawyer, took a similar stand, forfeiting matches he was scheduled to play against Alabama. "Playing girls against men makes a monkey show out of tennis," he said.

The college picture isn't much rosier in the seventies than it was in the fifties. Carin Cone, the 1956 Olympic backstroke champion, recalls looking around for a college that offered swimming. "I wrote to Duke, and the director of admissions replied, 'You're fully qualified academically to enroll at Duke. As to that interesting hobby of yours, our women's pool is open from 5 to 6 P.M. on Tuesdays and Thursdays.'"

Women's access to basketball courts still follows the same sorry pattern. As of 1971, for example, the State University of New York at Cortland allotted only *half of one* of its six basketball courts to women players.

In sport, as everywhere, money talks. But in women's collegiate athletic programs, it barely whispers. The discrepancy between male and female athletic budgets at most colleges is monumental.

At UCLA the annual allocation for men's sports is $2.9 million; for women's $20,000. In 1964, gold medal Olympic swimmers Donna de Varona and Marilyn White, both UCLA students, entered as unaffiliated competitors because their university had no separate swimming program for women. There is one now, and swimming is one of ten sports offered to women at UCLA. Men have eighteen.

Scholarships for the department's 811 male athletes total $498,000, and another $408,000 is divided among 31 full-time male coaches. But the ten coaches who work with UCLA's 175 women athletes are not paid. And they have no funds at all for recruiting.

Shirley Johnson, a former track teammate of Wilma Rudolph at Texas A&M, is trying to expand the women's sport program at UCLA. But during her seven years as head of the program, little has changed. Johnson's salary is taken out of the $20,000 budget, and she occupies a single desk in the bustling office of intramural sports.

"Most money goes for equipment, travel expenses, officials, everyday necessities," she told a *Los Angeles Times* reporter. "None is spent on recruiting or athletic scholarships. All [women's] coaches are full-time students, faculty, or staff who coach in their off-hours."

Two years ago Johnson appealed and changed a rule barring male coaches from women's athletics. One of the three men now in the department, twenty-two-year-old basketball player Dave Katz, says, "Women's basketball is at a pretty high level of competition. The ability of some of our guards is equal to that of a lot of varsity men." But, he adds, "The attitude around here toward girls is half snotty, like it's some kind of a joke. We're never allowed to practice in Pauley Gymnasium, even though we play our games there."

At Western Michigan University the women's athletic department has to make ends meet on a $2000-per-year budget. Students practice in a run-down gymnasium with ancient uniforms and equipment. When the WMU women's volleyball team won the state championship, supporters had to solicit private contributions to pay the team's way to the national playoff.

At the University of Maine, the women's athletic program gets $18,000 out of a total athletics budget of half a million—despite the fact that both programs are supported through activity fees paid by male and female students. The men's program also gets an outsize share of the gate receipts from baseball and football games, along with most of the publicity from the public-relations office (which is separately funded).

At Western Illinois University, student activity fees support a $10,000 women's program, while the men get $120,000. Yet women make up more than half of the student body and pay for more than half of the seats sold at football, basketball, and hockey games.

The story is pretty much the same all over the country. Until women achieve financial equality in collegiate sports, they'll continue to get the short end in other respects.

Coaching, for instance. New training techniques, which have a lot to do with record-breaking performances by male athletes (including Mark Spitz's recent victories), are simply not available to the majority of sportswomen.

When men do coach women athletes, their approach is often male-oriented. "Men teach muscle golf," says Carol Mann, women's golfing champion. "Women know they don't have the edge on strength, but they can achieve the same things if they're trained properly."[6]

"Women have very few places where they can receive any real instruction or coaching in athletics," says Micki Scott of the Institute for the Study of Sport and Society at Oberlin. "I've watched dozens of women's track meets, and it's incredible what talent exists that's been left untrained and uncoached."

"It's a vicious circle," UCLA coach and women's Olympic trainer Jim Bush told UPI reporter Lucinda Franks. "Women get poor training and then never have a chance to improve through competition, because promoters don't want to enter athletes who have been improperly trained. It destroys spectator interest, and they lose money."[7]

Taboos against feminine competition have been particularly effective, operating as they do on at least three levels.

On the first level, women are emotionally conditioned against physical competition, persuaded that it is not only "unfeminine" but somehow impolite. Accustomed to supporting male egos, they even take a supportive attitude toward women when competing with them outside the perimeters of the femininity game.

Micki Scott recalls feeling sorry for a slow friend in a California six-mile run. "For a while we were running side by side," she says. "Then I noticed she was getting tired, and I just couldn't bring myself to leave her behind. So I dropped back and paced her."

Says 1964 Olympic swimmer Ginny Duenkel: "Girls aren't conditioned to give it everything they've got. I've always noticed that women are never really tired after a swimming event, but most of the men are absolutely wrung out. I'd like to see how well women could do if they really turned it on."

On another level, women have been persuaded that their strength and endurance will decline with age. They see the records being set by thirteen- and fourteen-year-olds, and they are discouraged socially from further competition—so they drop out. "The drive was gone, and there was no motivation to keep trying," says Pat Kelly Jacobson, former Connecticut state and national swimming champion who is now an author and illustrator. "At school I was treated like a freak, particularly by the boys. To stay on top I would have had to practice long hours, and I just didn't have it in me."

A few years ago, at the age of thirty-four, Jacobson came in three lengths ahead of competitors at an otherwise all-male meet for employees of the large corporation where her husband works. "It was a relay, and they put their best swimmers on my team, figuring I'd do badly," she says. "It really surprised the opposition to see me sitting on the edge of the pool waiting for them to arrive. I wouldn't say they were exactly happy about it."

Statistical differences in men's and women's sports occur partly because few *older* women are competing. Male records are generally set by seventeen- and eighteen-year-olds. Says swimming coach Buck Dawson: "Girls' records would be a lot better if they stayed with it, but they're threatened by social disapproval and they drop out."

Emotional pressure and scientific propaganda against women in sport are combined on yet another level by men like Paul Weiss, our friend from chapter 4:

"Men are able to live in their bodies only if they are taught and trained to turn their minds into bodily vectors," Weiss intones. "And they can become excellent in and through their bodies only if they learn to identify themselves with their bodies and what these do. Normal women do not have this problem, at least in the acute form it presents to man."

One wonders on what authority Weiss speaks—apparently only his own, with a little help from Freud. His opinions will come as a surprise to a lot of women. For instance, women "do not have as strong a need as men to see what it is their bodies can do, in part because they are more firmly established in their roles as social beings, wives, and mothers than the men are in their roles."

And there's more: "Despite her . . . flights of fancy," says Weiss, a woman "is less abstract than a man because her mind is persistently ordered toward bodily problems. . . . Where a man might be proud of his body, she is proud *in* her body; where he uses it, she lives it as a lure. . . . Where a young man spends his time redirecting his mind and disciplining his body, she has only the problem of making it function more gracefully and harmoniously than it natively can and does."

Blacks have rhythm. Women have native grace and harmony.

The effect on women of such combined medical and philosophical arguments is almost insurmountable. Add the fact that most girls are discouraged from achievement, and you begin to understand why most women won't even try to compete. Those that do usually can't take the pressure after the age of sixteen or seventeen and give up.

The fact that far fewer women than men compete also holds women's records down. Winning time improves in direct proportion to the number of participants in a given event. If you have ten thousand swimmers competing nationally in the 100-meter freestyle, for instance, the top time obviously will be better than it would be if only two hundred swimmers competed. And thousands more men than women compete in sports at every level.

Only when women have competitive and numerical equality, equal financing and coaching, can it be determined how well they actually stand up against men in speed, endurance, and strength. As it is, they've done pretty well.

In the 1972 Olympics, Ludmila Bragina of Russia ran the metrical equivalent of the four-minute mile—matching the national collegiate male record of fifteen years ago. And 1972 was the first year that women had been allowed to compete in the 1500 meters. In 1952 Marjorie Jackson won the 100-meter race in 11.5 seconds; ten years later Wilma Rudolph did it in 11.3; and in 1968, Wyomia Tyus did it in 11. (Men's gold medalist James Hines was only 1.1 seconds faster).

But according to people like Ralph Schoenstein, it's all a waste of time. "A look at the track records shows that the fastest woman in the world, statuesque twenty-six-year-old Chi Cheng of Taiwan, has run the 100-yard dash in ten seconds flat," he says in that *Seventeen* article. "Hundreds of men, however, have already matched Chi Cheng's time; half the ends in football can do it. . . ."

The exaggeration is gross. There are some men—a select few drafted from among thousands of competitors for the pro football leagues—who are able to match this time. "But certainly not hundreds," says Jay Weiner, of the Institute for the Study of Sport in Society. And remember that in the 100-meter run, we are talking about a record difference of only 1.1 seconds between male and female competitors.

It's time men stopped running women down with feeble comparisons intended to make men look unmatchable if not invincible. One of these days the physical supremacists are going to get run out of town.

6

BLOOMER GIRLS, TOMBOYS, AND YANKEE DOODLE DANDIES

> Every girl, it seems, has a large store of vital and
> nervous energy upon which to draw in the great
> crisis of motherhood. If the foolish virgin uses up
> this deposit in daily expenditures on the hockey field
> or tennis court, as a boy can afford to, then she
> is left bankrupt in her great crisis and her children
> have to pay the bill. . . .
>
> "College Sports and Motherhood"
> *New York Times Book Review*
> July 3, 1921

American women haven't always been left out of sports.
In fact, the two decades before 1920 were in some ways
a golden age for women's athletics. The feminist movement
begun in the nineteenth century was gathering momentum;
and women's sports, which had become increasingly
popular, were not yet under the control of the men's Amateur
Athletic Union. In those days women went all out for
sport—even out on a limb:

"One of the most curious shots in golf was made today
at the Crawfordsville (Indiana) Country Club course,"
reported the *New York Times* in August 1922. "Mrs. Galen

Blackford, society matron and semifinalist in the women's golf tournament, calmly climbed a tree and played a mashie niblic approach from a bird's nest. . . . Her shot went clean on to the green for a halved hole. . . ."

At that time, intercollegiate and high school competitions for girls drew impressive crowds and coverage, as did professional women's events. News stories hailed the careers of prodigies like May Sutton, who took the Pacific Southwest tennis championship at thirteen and went on four years later to win the national championship and two successive victories at Wimbledon. Or Eleanor Sears, a Boston society girl who campaigned against male domination in sports and made headlines with her victories in tennis, golf, rifle shooting, swimming, and squash.

Dr. Tenley Albright, the 1957 Olympic figure-skating champion, who has studied this period in sports extensively, believes that women in sports were both more active and more accepted at the turn of the century than they are today.

What happened to this golden age of women's participation? Very much the same thing that caused the ancient Greek Olympics to become corrupt and misogynistic 2400 years before. Thanks to a combination of war, commerce, and philosophy, sport became a male obsession in America—at which point, not surprisingly, women were kicked out of it. Though the Olympics had begun as a time of truce and a respite from war, this tradition came to an end after the Persian invasions of Thermopylae and Salamis in 480 B.C., when talented amateurs were forced to forego the games in favor of defending their commercial interests. Men who went to the games in those war years were professional athletes—like the boxer Theogenes, who won all the crowns in 480 B.C. and held the title for twenty-two years.[1]

By the end of the fifth century, Euripides was deriding

the "tribe of athletes," and Aristotle was contrasting *athletes* to *idiotes*—which then meant the ordinary amateur. A century later, money prizes were being offered at athletic events throughout the Mediterranean world, and professional athletes were able to earn a good living. At the same time, wealthy patrons were furthering their political and commercial careers by sponsoring athletic events.

Similar factors were operative in America in the early nineteen-twenties. The Industrial Revolution, which had made war profitable as well as political, had also made possible for the first time the outfitting, transport, and promotion of national professional sports teams. Farm-oriented recreation for all was now replaced by urban-based, spectator events staged by professional teams. And when World War I began, the public attitude toward sport changed. Thereafter sport was associated with patriotism and machismo—a preparation for war and an affirmation of the American way.

Until the nineteen-twenties—in fact, since the beginning of the nineteenth century—women had slowly been gaining physical as well as intellectual rights. Early Victorian women had put up with ice skating in long skirts and riding to hounds side saddle, preserving their feminine image at the risk of their necks. But by the time of the American Civil War, girls' schools began offering limited athletic programs of mild calisthenics, dancing, and "physically taxing domestic duties."[2]

The Seneca Falls Women's Rights convention in 1848 had little immediate, nationwide impact on this curriculum—or, indeed, on approval of women's education in general. Despite the successful debut of several women's colleges, the president of Harvard was still wondering in 1870 whether an academic education was beneficial to women's health and development. Around the same time, the Reverend John

Todd of Boston asked, "Is it certain that the delicate nervous physical organization of women is such (I admit all you ask as to her quickness of mind and fine mental attributes) that she can endure the physical strain requisite for a regular, old-fashioned college course?"[3]

Nevertheless, by 1865 at least one college, Vassar, was offering its students calisthenics, riding, boating, swimming, skating . . . and gardening. Smith girls, who were limited during the same period to marching, throwing bean bags, drilling with wands, and exercising to Strauss waltzes on the Victrola, were one up on Vassar by 1890—dribbling and shooting baskets.

Though one usually thinks of basketball as a men's sport, it was introduced by Sarah Berenson to the Smith College program right after the game was invented in the eighteen-eighties. "The value of athletic sports for men is not questioned," she wrote in her book *Basketball for Women* (1894). "It's a very different matter, however, when we speak of athletics for women. Until very recent years, the so-called ideal woman was a small-waisted, small-footed, small-brained damsel who prided herself on her delicate health, who thought fainting interesting and hysterics fascinating."[4]

It would be comforting—and naïve—to think that the passage of nearly eighty years has made a substantial difference in most college physical-education departments' attitude toward women's athletics. As we saw in the last chapter, it hasn't.

Athletic policies had always been more liberal at Western and some Midwestern colleges, where women had a tradition of toughness. At the University of Wisconsin in 1890, for instance, girls were bowling and playing coed tennis and ice hockey. Western women had always been more physically self-reliant than their Eastern sisters; they had to be to withstand the rigors of frontier life. In fact, the word "tomboy" originated in the West, as a *complimentary* term for a woman who could do a man's work. The so-called "feminization" of the West occurred after the Gold Rush, when prostitutes were imported in large numbers to consort with successful Forty-niners. "Tomboys" were scarce, and they were working too hard to do much carousing, so it was ladies of the evening who rose to social prominence and became the founding matriarchs of much of California society.[5]

Toward the end of the nineteenth century, a new sport came on the scene that caused a countrywide revolution among women. The modern safety bicycle was invented, and women in the United States and in Europe abandoned their hoop skirts and started pedaling around in pants. Amelia Bloomer's Turkish pantaloons, which she had tried unsuccessfully to introduce at mid-century but which had caught on only in the Oneida Community, suddenly became chic.

"Had it not been for the extraordinary vogue which bicycling has had for the past two years in London and Paris," wrote Dr. Elizabeth Mitchell in 1896, "we should still be wearing hoops."[6]

The full Turkish trousers, nipped in at the ankle and covered by a knee-length overskirt, were a radical departure from hoop skirts. But as one cyclist of the time put it: "On the bicycle excursion, a special adaptation of dress is absolutely necessary; for skirts, while they have not hindered women from climbing to the topmost branches of education, may prove fatal in downhill coasting."

Elizabeth Cady Stanton saw more than sartorial significance in the new sport: "Many a woman," she wrote, "is riding to suffrage on a bicycle."[7]

The general public, however, was less than enthusiastic

about the new fad; in fact, it was outraged. "Bicycling tends to destroy the sweet simplicity of a woman's girlish nature," warned one writer in 1897. "Besides, how dreadful it would be if, by some accident, she were to fall off into the arms of a strange man."

The Women's Rescue League of America, a service organization, flatly predicted disaster. The new sport, they foresaw, would lead women into immoral and indecent behavior and make them unfit for childbearing. The League took action: "Whereas bicycling by young women has helped to swell the ranks of reckless girls who finally drift into the standing army of outcast women of the U.S., more than any other medium . . . therefore, be it resolved that the Women's Rescue League petition all true women and clergymen to aid in denouncing the present bicycle craze by women as indecent and vulgar."

The Canadian press leaped to the bicyclists' defense: "Elderly ladies in jaunty hats and irreproachable leggings strike their miniature alarm bells with dowagerlike demeanor and enter the stream of wheel life with all the nerve of veterans," read the *Manitoba Free Press*. "The indolence of declining responsibility has gone; the charm of being a nerveless nonentity has gone; instead there is the woman who has thrown off the shackles of foolishness and pluckily grasped a power for health and pleasure."[8]

By the turn of the century, the bicycling Bloomer girls had been joined by the Gibson Girls, who played tennis and hockey in skirts raised daringly to the ankle.

Then along came speed demon Henry Ford, who hired Barney Oldfield, a bicycle racer with a reputation for not being afraid of anything, to test-drive his four-cylinder, eighty-horsepower "999."

Blanche Scott wasn't afraid of anything, either. In 1910

she set a new precedent for women, driving an Overland from New York to San Francisco. A few months later she took her reputation into the air. Though male aviators had done their best to keep women grounded, they couldn't keep Blanche Scott down. Over the objections of Glenn Curtiss, then the titan of American aviation, Scott took off on her maiden flight at the Hammondsport Flying Field. Soon she was known as "America's Flying Bloomer Girl."

"Glenn Curtiss was mad," Scott recalled. "In fact, he was absolutely livid about sweet little me learning to fly. A birdwoman in that day and age? Never."[9]

Certainly Blanche Scott's feat failed to convince the "experts" that women were suited for such adventures. In 1912, *Outing* magazine contended that differences in reaction time (sound familiar?) made them unfit to fly:

"Other things being equal," read the *Outing* editorial, "the man who has had the most experience in outdoor sport should be the best aviator. By the same token, women should be barred. . . . Women haven't the background of games of strength that men have. Their powers of correlation are correspondingly limited, and their ability to cope with sudden emergency is inadequate."

Reaction time failed to slow down women like Elinor Smith and Jacqueline Cochrane. Elinor Smith, who made her solo flight at age fifteen, set a women's endurance record at Roosevelt Field in 1929 when she spent 26 hours and 21 minutes in the air at an altitude of 30,000 feet. She passed out for five miles of the flight—not because of physical frailty but because her oxygen tank failed. And she managed to bring her plane down safely despite an engine failure that left her with a dead throttle and nearly sent her into the wires.

And Jacqueline Cochrane, who won the Bendix transcontinental race against a field of all-male pilots in 1937, later became the first woman to fly a jet across the Atlantic and the first to exceed the speed of sound. In 1964, when she was in her late fifties, Cochrane established three new world speed records in Lockheed's F-104-G Starfighter.

Unfortunately, the positions taken by publications like *Outing* and by educators proved more influential than did the accounts of such exploits. These came, in fact, to be viewed as extraordinary if not freakish occurrences, outside the expectations of the average woman.

By 1917, when American entered World War I, educators were echoing Freud's views about sexual differences. And by 1923, these supposed differences were doing service as an excuse for the drastic curtailment of women's sport—and for its control by the Amateur Athletic Union. Meanwhile, male professional sport—thanks mostly to the First World War—took the chauvinistic direction it still follows today.

This response in America in some ways paralleled the attitude of the Germans, who viewed sport as had the Romans—seeing it not as a respite from war but as a substitute and preparation for it. By World War II, General von Reichenau had designated war as the "noblest sport of all." Germany had been requiring calisthenics as part of school curricula ever since Friedrich Jahn invented them in 1811. American boys, on the other hand, had been encouraged to emulate Horatio Alger's heroes at the expense of their physical strength. When the first American troops hit the beaches of France in 1917, it immediately became apparent that they were badly out of shape. A subsequent report by the provost marshal revealed that of the three million American men drafted, one million were physically unfit for military duty.

Calisthenics were summarily introduced as part of military basic training, and Congress appropriated funds to establish physical education departments in the public schools. Thereafter, sport became irretrievably patriotic. Fitness was something to be achieved through sacrifice, suffering, and discipline; playing games was something one did to win. America, by God, was going to shape up. And she was going to go about it in a singularly intense and humorless way.

Thus began the deification of the athlete—still, for many Americans, the epitome of patriotism and the masculine ideal—which apparently reached its zenith in the astronaut. Only athletic patriots could make it to the moon (male patriots, that is).

Women, left out of the patriotic trend in sports from the beginning, were also deprived of the fun of athletic competition. Calisthenics, instead, was ruled the acceptable way for women to shape up. "Physical educators emphasized conditioning programs for women who entered industry," C. W. Hackensmith writes in his *History of Physical Education*, "and for those who wanted to be fit because it was patriotic."[10]

Before this period, doctors had set what policies there were for women's participation in sport. Now the educators took over. Emphasizing psychology more than physiology, they decreed that women were not suited for rugged competitive sport and that competition itself was psychologically damaging to women.

And so, despite the successes women were enjoying in international competition (they had been participating in the Olympics since 1912), everyone seemed to be fretting about whether or not they were up to it. In 1922, after a meet in Paris, several women competitors cried after being defeated. That provided an excuse for a convention of the Women's Athletic Congress at Vichy, which addressed itself to the effect of extensive athletic activity upon women's health, and adopted resolutions severely limiting some kinds of competition and suppressing others altogether.

In October of the same year, the National Recreation Congress passed a resolution deploring current policies of competitive sports for women. Young women (known in those days as sub-flappers) were advised instead to join the Camp Fire Girls. "The problem of the sub-flapper was touched on by Lester Scott, national secretary of the Camp Fire Girls," read a *New York Times* report of the NRC convention. "The programs of the CFG," he said, "with its nature study and outdoor activities, are satisfactory outlets for the sub-flapper's surplus energy."[11]

After members of the National Recreation Congress had passed the resolution on women's sports, said the *Times*, they "demonstrated their vital belief in the powers of recreation by playing leapfrog, ring-around-the-rosy, and other famous old games."

The movement to limit women's participation in sports continued to gain momentum, and in November 1922 the Amateur Athletic Union—a male organization—voted to assume control of women's athletics: "Through its efforts, state basketball tournaments for high school girls were eventually eliminated, intramural programs widely adopted . . . and the health supervision of participants improved."[12]

Within a few years, every state athletic association had adopted rules barring young women from competitive sport and, in some instances, established special "women's" rules. In basketball, for example, girls were restricted to the use of half the court and limited to three dribbles.

"We played high school basketball by boys' rules until 1922," recalls Adelaide Hawley, who for fifteen years portrayed Betty Crocker on television and radio. "When they changed to the new girls' rules, we all quit the team. It wasn't fun any more."

The feminine-competition backlash wasn't limited to the sports world. Early in 1923, when the Equal Rights Amendment came before Congress, it was put into committee—where it stayed for nearly half a century—by Emanuel Celler.

"There is no equality except in a cemetery," he said then. "There are differences in physical structure and biological function. . . . There is more difference between male and female than between a horse chestnut and a chestnut horse."[13]

And so, three years after they won the vote, women's bid for other equal rights had been shelved—and their right to establish their own athletic policies had been taken away.

7

THE MASCULINITY RITE

For when the One Great Scorer comes
To write against your name,
He marks—not that you won or lost—
But how you played the game.
　　　　　　　　Grantland Rice, c. 1905

Winning isn't everything. It's the
only thing.
　　　　　　　　Vince Lombardi, c. 1967

Men have gone to a lot of trouble to keep women out of competitive sport. Legislators have written laws about it. Physicians and anthropologists have published scholarly papers about it. Philosophers and educators have pros-elytized about it. Why all the hubbub over mere games?

The answer is that games and sport are not "mere"—not just an "amusement or diversion," as Webster defines them; not extracultural but intrinsic social and individual processes that shape human behavior. At its best, sport can be a positive reinforcement of youthful goals and ideals. At its worst, it is a vicious reinforcement of the worst goals of society as well· as a reflection of them. And the worst can be seen in professional sport today.

Conditioned against involvement in competitive sport, women are often bored and frequently repelled by the violence and corruption of the professional sports scene. Yet an understanding of this male-dominated world—and how it evolved into such a spectacle—is important. For sport is a basic part of the system the new feminists are challenging, a sort of subcellar to the male ego and a reflection of the world at large. Sport is a microcosm in which prejudice, discrimination, attitudes, and ideals are magnified. A closer look at it should give women a clearer picture of where they are in real life, why they're there, and what changes are needed.

Pro sport and, all too often, amateur sport are no longer play but work, not relaxing but anxiety-ridden, not a test of prowess but a proof of maleness and an often corrupt contest for personal wealth, not an outlet for but a contributing cause of aggression—in short, the mirror image of male activities in politics, in industry, and on the battlefield.

"It would be impossible for me not to see football as both a reflection and reinforcement of the worst things in American culture," writes Dave Meggyesy, former linebacker for the St. Louis Cardinals, in *Out of Their League*. "There was the incredible racism which I was to see close up in the Cardinals' organization and throughout the League. There was also the violence and sadism, not so much on the part of the players or in the game itself, but very much in the minds of the beholders—the millions of Americans who watch football every weekend in something approaching a sexual frenzy.

"And then there was the whole militaristic aura surrounding pro football, not only in obvious things like football stars visiting troops in Vietnam, but in the language of the game—'throwing the bomb,' being a 'field general,' etc., and in the unthinking obligation to 'duty' required by the players. In short, the game has been wrapped in red, white, and blue. . . ."

Grantland Rice's poetic sentimentality is a relic of another age. It's the late Lombardi who was on the ball: It's not how you play the game, but whether you win, period. Losing is a national nightmare; winning, an obsession. The end justifies the means, whether it involves sticking a thumb in somebody's eye, trying to sabotage a national election, or defoliating a countryside and maiming a generation of children. (Early in 1972, when a University of Michigan survey revealed that 65 per cent of Americans wanted out of Vietnam, it was discovered that half of this number were motivated not by compassion but by disgust that our military quarterbacks hadn't called a winning play.[1])

If battles are won on playing fields, playing fields have become miniature battlegrounds. Divisions between sport and reality have become ominously blurred. Things have reached a point where our Commander-in-Chief phones football coaches at 1 A.M. to suggest alternate plays for the next game and constantly draws parallels between the White House and the gridiron:

"This game affects the life of the nation and the world," President Nixon recently said of the presidency and public office to *New York Times* reporter Saul Pett. "For that reason an individual, whether he's a President or a member of Congress or the Senate or Cabinet must play the game . . . right up to the hilt. . . . The worst thing you can do is to relax, to let up. . . . The Redskins were relaxed in their last game of the regular season and they were flat and they got clobbered."[2]

The game Nixon spoke of was evoked in a more sinister light during James W. McCord's testimony on the second day of the Senate hearings on Watergate. Recalling efforts by Treasury Department official John Caulfield to persuade him to plead guilty and remain silent in return for executive clemency, convicted burglar McCord said Caulfield told him: "Everybody else is on track but you. You are not following the game plan. You seem to be pursuing your own course of action. Do not talk if called before the grand jury. Keep silent and do the same if called before a congressional committee . . . you are fouling up the game plan."

Competitive sport, which should have so much to offer, has become a sorry model for youthful behavior and a vicious reinforcement of the masculinity trap.

"Among children the tendency toward irrational competition increases with age," wrote L. Nison and Spencer Kagan in the September 1972 issue of *Psychology Today*. "And we can easily find adults whose drive to compete overrides self-interest—in academia, athletics, business, politics, and Vietnam."

Outside the Olympics, as sociologist Alex Natan has noted, international competitive sport has become a playground for ideologies, mirroring the political tensions of the world and its industrial interests as well:

"The terrible accidents at the Le Mans twenty-four-hour motorcar race at the Mille Miglia did not prevent any competitor from completing the course—because the rivalry of the car industries was at stake," Natan has written. "In the communist countries the Commissar for Sport has full control and may encourage the making of records, even under the threat of reprisal. . . . In South Africa, no colored man has the remotest chance of entering even the trial contests for the national team selection. On the other hand, Ghana and Nigeria will hardly allow any white men on their teams. . . . In South America, barbed wire fences must be put up for the protection of visiting foreign players from the wrath of infuriated nationalism. . . ."[3]

Competition has gone haywire. Instead of competing to improve skills and judge them against others, men compete only to win. The implications of this either/or approach—in life and in sport—are grim. "An essential aspect of creativity is not being afraid to fail," Dr. Edwin Land of Polaroid told a *Life* reporter last year. "Scientists make it permissible to fail repeatedly until in the end they get the result they wanted. . . . [Yet] the first time you fail outside the scientific world you are through." (October 27, 1972)

But in sport, as in other areas of life, the American male faces only two alternatives—winning or losing, success or failure. As a spectator, his personal sense of self-esteem, like the national one, depends on backing the winning teams. For a time the New York Mets *were* the American dream—the losers who rose to take the pennant. And Joe Namath is still the ultimate in machismo, the racy renegade who handles women and linebackers with equal panache.

The winner-loser syndrome has paralyzed the average American male into passive spectatordom. Because sport has become a way of life instead of a useful, diverting rehearsal for it, the stakes are too high for most men to afford. It's safer for men to appoint surrogates to win for them while they watch the contest over a glass of beer.

Even *Glamour* magazine has recognized the peculiar male addiction to sport, recently devoting a column of advice to women about it: "Sports can simplify the complexities of a man's life because they always have a winner and a loser," says the editorial. "A man tends to identify with one of them and feel optimistic whether his team wins or loses, since there's always hope that even a losing team may come out on top eventually."[4]

Glamour was right to see sports as a microcosm, wrong about the optimism. When your life is passing in front of you, it's hard to be optimistic in defeat.

"You guys didn't want to win bad enough. You're a bum," a fan yelled at linebacker Mike Montler after the New England Patriots lost a game in the fall of 1972. Later, in his office high above Shaefer Stadium, Patriot's manager Dan Marcotte got a play-by-play account (via walkie-talkie) of the fans' postgame antics: "The fans are starting to throw things at the players. . . . They're throwing full beer cans . . . tearing up the chairs in the south stands. . . ."

Earlier, Howeard Berk, vice president for administration at Yankee Stadium, had told a *National Observer* reporter: "When the Giants are winning, everyone is happy, and it's festive. But if we're losing or, worse, losing badly—it's awful."[5]

The strain on male spectators is nothing compared to what the athletes themselves go through. Each game a pro plays, says Oberlin's Jack Scott, indeed becomes a masculinity rite—with the coach as chief shaman.

"Most coaches quickly learn that their chief motivational tool is the dispensation of manhood," Scott has written. "The successful coach is usually the one who can keep the athletes so insecure that they are continually trying to prove their [virility]. . . . The late Vince Lombardi had the players of the Green Bay Packers convinced that to lose a football game was to lose one's manhood.

"It is for this reason that coaches themselves are so obsessed with being real men—straight from the square-jawed, character-armored John Wayne mold. If the coach is going to grant others their masculinity, he, of course, must be the personification of all a man is supposed to be. . . . The most complimentary remark a coach can make about a male athlete is to call him a real stud or animal, and the most derogatory . . . to intimate the athlete may be effeminate."[6]

Psychoanalyst Morton Golden believes that many male spectators suffer from the same sexual insecurity. "A man may watch sports because of doubts and anxieties within himself," he writes. "Many men sublimate their aggressive sexual desires by identifying with the aggressive, idolized athletic hero."[7]

If, as Jack Scott says, being compared to a woman is the most derogatory thing that can be said about an athlete, what does this say about femininity? Men are obviously contemptuous of "feminine" behavior, even as they anxiously seek to perpetuate it. Femininity is apparently an essential prop in the masculinity rite, a point of contrast against which male behavior can be measured and virility reaffirmed. Women are fall guys for the featured performers; when they step out of this role, the leading men feel threatened.

With so much male ego riding on every game, it obviously wouldn't do to see a woman anywhere near home plate. Bernice Gera got behind it for a while—after winning a long legal battle—as the first woman umpire in the minor leagues. After one game, she quit in disgust. "The men just wouldn't cooperate," she said. "It wasn't worth the hassle."

The male monopoly on contact sport even extends to the press box, where a woman's only risk of injury is from the men who try to keep her out. In the spring of 1972, Helen Lippincott, a part-time reporter for *Newsweek* magazine, was barred from the press box at San Francisco's Candlestick Park. Despite her walletful of press credentials, two burly guards insisted that she move to the bleachers.

"We don't care what the Supreme Court says," the bouncers told her. "We don't care what state law says. Women are not allowed in the press box. . . . Leave quietly or we'll bump you out on your ass."[8]

In the fall of 1972, former CBS sportscaster Lee Arthur was denied access to the Oakland Raiders' practice field. After asking her to leave, head coach John Madden said, "Why don't you women stay home and be lovers and leave TV and football to the men?"

"Presently there are only three women I know of working successfully in the sportscasting field," Arthur told a recent NOW convention. "There's Jane Chastain in Miami, Jeannie Morris in Chicago, and Juliette Ashdown in Atlanta. . . . None of these women have their own sports shows."[9]

Arthur added that CBS has, over the years, attempted unsuccessfully to increase its female audience on the Sunday NFL football pregame show by using a woman on a portion of it. "For two seasons, first Jean Parr, then Carol Howie covered such topics as why football players use black smears under their eyes and how much food is consumed by a team during a week at training camp. . . . The third season, they hired football writer Elinor Kaine, who *knew* football. She lasted only one season—her controversial treatment of football and gossip items ruffled feathers on several football teams. Elinor got married and moved to France."

Before her marriage, she sued the Giants, the Jets, and the Yale Bowl for not allowing women into football press boxes. Though Kaine won the suit, Lee Arthur says it's still rare to see a woman in a press box. "So much so that when I was in the Miami Dolphins' press box, a black scout grinned and said 'Man, they're letting everybody in now. First blacks, now women. Where will it end?'"[10]

Not only press boxes but dugouts, ringsides, pit stops at racetracks, even press association parties are off limits to women. (In January 1973, *Sports Illustrated* writer Stephanie

Salter was asked to leave the annual Baseball Writers' Association dinner.)

Professionalism in sport has made it doubly difficult for women to break down any of the barriers. Pro sport is no longer just a means to an end but an end in itself, the job and the masculinity rite rolled into one. In the past, an amateur sportsman might win a Rhodes scholarship and go on to become a leader in industry or in politics. Today, he's drafted into the big leagues. When sport becomes bread and butter, women can expect the same reaction to feminine intrusion that they used to find on the assembly line.

A woman athlete trying to get on a pro team would face not only prejudice but regulatory barriers backed up by great economic power and political influence. In his book *They Call It a Game,* Bernie Parrish calls oil and food tycoon H. L. Hunt the "sugar daddy of the AFL." Bud Adams of the Ada Oil Company (Phillips 66) owns the Houston Oilers; oil baron John Mecom gave his son the New Orleans Saints as a present. And Clint Murchison owns and runs the Dallas Cowboys with a distinguished board of directors that includes Senators J. Howard Edmondson (Democrat of Oklahoma) and Clinton P. Anderson (Democrat of New Mexico).

Many of the owners, Parrish reveals, treat football teams a lot like oil wells on their tax returns. Clint Murchison reported $430,000 in income from the Cowboys in 1967, which Parrish found to be a fraction of the real earnings. After doing a lot of digging, he discovered that in 1970 the total income of the Cowboys was in excess of $135 million. Parrish concluded: "With a player payroll of less than 20 per cent of the gross income, with no raw materials or manufacturing machinery to buy, no factories to build and maintain and only small research and development costs, since the colleges hand the pros a highly refined product free of charge . . . no business ever had it so good or bilked the public so badly."

The Supreme Court ruled in 1957 that pro football was a business and therefore subject to antitrust laws. But baseball, in which the league setup is essentially the same, is exempt. And pro baseball, like football, has become a monopoly, tied in financially—in a blurry corporate maze—to television, broadcasting, and newspaper interests, as well as to hundreds of corporations and businesses.

Organized crime is also making a bundle out of pro sport. In a 1965 *Esquire* article, Ovid Demaris reckons the take somewhere in the neighborhood of $13.3 billion in gambling. Witnesses in the 1970 congressional hearings put it almost four times higher: at $50 billion. Games can be—and, according to Parrish and Demaris, often are—easily fixed.

In America, professional sport has paralleled the growth of industry and technology—becoming as corrupt and commercial as the society it reflects. And because pro sport and modern society have both prospered in the name of competition, competition itself has ended up with a bad name. A liberal reaction against the sort of cutthroat competition associated with the worst aspects of free enterprise has existed since the nineteen-twenties.

Some educators—many of them women—subsequently acquired an aversion to what competition had come to represent, concluding that it is inherently destructive and therefore to be avoided. Certainly the materialistic, political, even violent direction competition has taken is deplorable. And this direction—in combination with all the subtler pressures discouraging women from competing—is often a persuasive last straw.

Excellence in any field is achieved only through competition, through trying to surpass the previous achievements of others or of oneself. "Competition is nature's law to ensure . . . specific superiority for progressive change," Ernest Remits has written. "History is largely an ominous record of man's intolerant adherence to fictitious superiority."[11]

The status of women has always been one of the more unfortunate effects of this "intolerant adherence" to mythical superiority. And one of the ways women can change it is to get out and compete—not only to win, but to develop skills and match those skills against others'.

"When Arthur Ashe plays tennis," says Dr. Edwin Land of Polaroid, "his purpose each day is to play the game in a way he has never played it before. It may be a backhand he uses, one that may never have been used before in that circumstance. His play is a fresh integration of his world at the instant of action. A really great scientist has the whole past at his disposal. At any instant he is rebuilding the world, molecule by molecule, in his subconscious. That is what you want in an athlete or a scientist." (*Life,* October 27, 1972)

Competition takes many forms: not just one team against another but one individual against another, against himself —or against nature. Competitive needs vary in every person. But everyone needs some extravocational competitive outlet, something to improve at, to excel in—whether it's showing dogs or showing off on water skis.

Former national and Olympic fencing champion Terry Terhune, now a university administrator, puts it this way: "Competing provides a valuable set of experiences to fall back on in my job. In sport I realized that I'd have good and bad days, that I could learn to overcome what appeared to be insurmountable obstacles."

Men are supposed to have an edge on competitive spirit. They're supposed to be more aggressive in team play, readier to accept the challenge of natural obstacles and the unknown.

Girls in school learn about Columbus, Hillary, Chichester, and Piccard. They memorize Tennyson's "Ulysses" (JFK's favorite poem):

> Yet all experience is an arch wherethrough
> Gleams that untravelled world, whose margin fades
> For ever and for ever when I move.

The goal is

> To strive, to seek, to find, and not to yield.

Well, many women feel that way too. For statistical proof we can turn to a recent study reported in the October 1971 issue of *Psychology Today:* "Women competitors show more creativity than their male counterparts. They are more reserved and cool, more experimental, more independent than males. . . . We attribute this to the cultural repression of women. To succeed in any field, a woman has to be able to stand up and spit in the eye of those in charge."[12]

As living proof, there are women like Shirley Bridges (wife of Harry Bridges, the oil executive, not the longshoreman), who took up mountain climbing after the age of forty, and is now one of the best climbers in the world—man or woman. She's climbed and skied in every major mountain range in the world, and was one of nine out of sixteen who managed to survive a particularly treacherous Himalayan climb.

Edmund Hillary climbed Everest "because it was there." In July 1971, Nicolette Milnes Walker, sailing a thirty-foot sloop, became the first woman to cross the Atlantic alone, "because I could find no reason for *not* going. . . . I wanted to do something which would not only give me intrinsic pleasure but would . . . bring in its wake further opportunities to change my whole life."

And, speaking of firsts, how many children—or adults —know that Jean F. Piccard wasn't alone on his historic ascent into the stratosphere? At the helm of the balloon as it soared aloft was Piccard's wife, Jeannette. She had her pilot's license; he didn't.

And few people know that John Fairfax wouldn't have survived "his" 361-day, 8000-mile rowboat voyage across the Pacific without Sylvia Cook, who comes off as definitely a secondary member of the trip in his accounts of it. Cook spent days alone at the oars, navigating at the edge of a cyclone while Fairfax lay delirious from a shark bite. In a story for *True* magazine, Fairfax refers to himself as a "professional adventurer," and to Cook as a temporary escapee from "a comfortable suburban life."

There are hundreds of women whose exploits are worth recording—but the records often aren't there. The editors of sports pages are men, and history is, for the most part, written for men by men, who either consciously or unconsciously want to perpetuate the idea that they are the only competitors worth mentioning.

It must have started somewhere, this business about women being suited for a sedentary indoor life while men are outside having all the adventures. But where? Some anthropologists would like to bury the blame in prehistory, where masculine and feminine natures supposedly diverged out of evolutionary necessity.

But the process is a lot more recent than that. It began not hundreds of thousands of years ago in the Pleistocene but less than three thousand years ago at the dawn of the Golden Age of Greece. And a closer look at that critical age yields a number of clues as to why men have turned into such bad sports—and why women have been left out of the game.

8

HOW THE GAME BEGAN

For we, we women, be not creatures cast
In diverse mold from men; to us is given
Such energy of life as stirs in them.
Eyes have we like to theirs, and limbs;
Throughout fashioned are we alike; one common light
We look on, and one common air we breathe;
With food are we nourished; nay, wherein
Have we been dowered of God more niggardly
Than men; Then let us shrink not from the fray!

Tisiphone
The Fall of Troy
Quintus Smyrnaeus[1]

The author of nature gave man strength of body and
intrepidity of mind to enable him to face great hardships,
and to woman was given a weak and delicate con-
stitution, accompanied by a natural softness and modest
timidity, which fit her for sedentary life.

Aristotle[2]

Most readings of history, recent or ancient,* leave the impression that the female body has largely existed only to be
clothed, admired, impregnated, confined, and buried. The

*The historical material which follows in this chapter is a brief summary of extensive
research done by Dr. Boslooper in primary sources of the literature of antiquity
and on works of art in museums. See Appendix II for selective references to the
artistic material cited and note references in the bibliography to ancient authors.

little that has been written about women in antiquity tends to ignore physical activities and focus instead on cultural and domestic roles.

There are no histories of women in sport. Books on the subject have been written by, for, and about men. The most one can find on athletic women of the past is an occasional chapter in books on the history of physical education, which presumably are read only by physical education majors.

Hundreds of sculptures, vases, and artifacts portraying physically active women exist, but most of them are locked up in museum storerooms. One notable exception—a bronze statue of an attractive and obviously female acrobat in the Metropolitan Museum of Art—is referred to in the accompanying text as "him."

In the world's leading museums, antique vases and household implements decorated with male and female figures in relief are usually displayed so that only their masculine side shows. When the curator of Greco-Roman antiquities at the British Museum in London was asked to explain this practice, he simply confirmed it: "The scenes of men fighting are shown to the public; what women are doing we put against the wall."

Books on the art of the Greco-Roman period virtually ignore the proliferation of available material on physically active women. As a result, few people realize that there was a period in the second millennium before Christ when woman's physical image was vastly different from what it is today.

The Amazons are the only ancient female athletes one hears about—and most women would probably rather not. The popular image of an Amazon is hardly flattering: a big, burly, single-breasted female; hostile, unattractive, a woman who has chosen to act like a man. This caricature originated in Golden Age Greece, where the Amazons in fact symbolized woman as she had been in an earlier period—strong and independent—an image that conflicted with the picture of woman the Greek philosophers sought to create. Ancient art and literature actually depicts the Amazons as fine-looking, skilled, and courageous—perhaps the last survivors of an ancient matriarchy that had thrived in the civilized world thousands of years before Christ during a period known as the Silver Age.

Many ancient and modern historians have dismissed the Amazons as figments of Greek imagination.[3] Some have interpreted the Amazon legends as allegories about the invasions of wild hordes from Asia—an external threat that had to be eradicated from a society already reeling from the thirty-year war with Sparta.

Actually the Amazons represented an internal force —comprising the once-powerful women of the ancient world—that had been driven to the fringes of society and was struggling to return. Elizabeth Gould Davis has described the gradual dissolution of this goddess-worshiping matriarchy around 1100 B.C., when the barbaric Dorians from the north invaded the Mediterranean world:

"It was they [the Dorians] who abolished goddess worship and set up shrines to Zeus and his family throughout Greece," she writes in *The First Sex*. "It was in Thrace, that land of mystery, that Zeus and the Dorians fought their first battles against the goddess, a fact which is memorialized in myth.

"During and after the invasion of the Dorians and the descent of Greece into temporary barbarism, the Silver Age was looked back upon with deep nostalgia as a time of peace and progress."[4]

The invaders brought with them superior iron weapons

(they introduced the Iron Age) and their male god Zeus and his pantheon. The succeeding centuries were a period of often violent transition to a patriarchal culture. But things had quieted down by the fifth century, and many of the great male thinkers of Athens were busy rationalizing the new patriarchy, erasing with sophistry the old image of woman. It was they who started the ugly rumors about Amazons and developed curious theories about women in general that continue to influence scholars today.

In both symbol and reality, then, the Amazons represented women who had once been active, strong, and independent. Men, unable to conquer them through superior intellect or physical strength, vanquished them through treachery, deception, faulty logic, and sheer force—a process recorded in both history and myth.[5]

The Greek historian Strabo[6] recounts two traditional histories of the Amazon women. One version places their home base in the northerly foothills of the Caucasus, the other in the mountains above Albania. Strabo says they spent much of their time plowing, planting, training horses, hunting, and practicing for war.

What did they look like? Strabo says they wore helmets, clothing, and girdles made from the skins of wild animals. A terracotta statuette of an Amazon has been described by Dietrich von Bothmer: "[She] wears white shoes with red soles, tied with purple thongs, purple trousers, a sleeved garment blue with red dots and red Attic helmet with violet cheek-pieces turned up and a white crest. Over her jacket she has a yellow leopard-skin with black spots . . . the Amazon carried a spear in her right hand . . . and a red quiver with a blue wave pattern along its edge hangs by her right side."[7]

"Amazon" means, literally, "without breasts." Legend

has it that the Amazon mothers cut off their daughters' right breasts in infancy to facilitate the use of bows, arrows, and spears; the left breast was supposedly left for suckling. This monomammarian image is *not* reflected in ancient sculptures, which portray Amazons as beautiful, tall, strong, and physically competent, similar to the athletic women of the Egyptian Old Kingdom, of Sparta, and of Minoan Crete. And all sculptures show them with both breasts intact.[8]

The concept of the one-breasted Amazon may have arisen because these women usually went into battle with quiver straps over their shoulders. Some observers may have assumed, because they couldn't see the right breast, that it wasn't there.

For two months every spring the Amazons were said to meet "in secrecy and darkness" with the Gargarians, a male tribe that lived in the Caucasus, to conceive their children. Female offspring of these brief liaisons were kept by the Amazons, while males were kept by the Gargarians and raised as their sons. Some ancient writers claim the Amazons killed their male offspring, but these are relatively late stories that could reflect the Hellenistic bias.

It seems reasonable to speculate that the Amazons represented the last vestiges of the ancient matriarchy. In the face of superior iron weapons (which Strabo said the Amazons later adopted and used in battle, fighting from horseback), some women may have retreated, seeking sanctuary in the mountains. From these fortresses, they may have made periodic forays into the Mediterranean area to try to regain a world that had once peacefully been theirs.

The historian Diodorus wrote that there were at least three different tribes of Amazon women.[9] And J. J. Bachofen has discovered references to the Amazonian tradition in the histories of all cultures: "They may be found from Central

Asia to the Occident, from the Scythian north to West Africa and beyond the ocean. . . . Everywhere Amazonianism is accompanied by violent acts of bloody vengeance against the male sex."[10]

Unable to win acceptance from men for their natural attributes and rights, the Amazons probably had a lot to avenge. Yet there is considerable evidence to suggest that they were fierce and hostile only in reaction to the barbarians who sought to oppress them. That the Amazons were, by nature, gentle is indicated in a passage from Plutarch: "The Amazons were naturally friendly to men and did not fly from Theseus when he touched upon their coasts but actually sent him presents, and he invited the one who brought them to come on board his ship; she came on board, and he put out to sea."[11]

The most famous mythical queen of the Amazons was Hippolyte, vanquished by Hercules in one of his great labors: "The ninth labour he enjoined on Hercules was to bring the belt of Hippolyte," says an account. "She was a queen of the Amazons, who dwelt about the Thermadon, a people great in war; for they cultivated the manly virtues, and if ever they gave birth to children through intercourse with the other sex, they reared the females. . . . Now Hippolyte had the belt of Ares in token of her superiority to all the rest. . . ."[12]

After her encounter with Hercules, Hippolyte was succeeded by Penthesileia, the last queen of the Amazons,[13] who was struck down by Achilles as she led her warriors to battle against the Greeks. All the contemporary accounts describe Penthesileia as a beautiful woman "with love-kindling eyes" and a ravishing smile. But her charm was lost on Achilles, who had heard—and believed—all those rumors about Amazons. Having entered the fray prepared to meet a broad-shouldered, single-breasted wonder, Achilles didn't pause to find out if his expectations tallied with reality. Rather than meet the queen in the customary hand-to-hand combat, he took aim from afar, caught Penthesileia off guard, and mortally wounded her with a javelin blow to the jugular.

The Fall of Troy gives an interesting account of how Achilles and his compatriots reacted as he strolled over to view his conquest:

> The Warriors gazed, and in their hearts
> They prayed
> That fair and sweet like her their wives
> Might seem,
> Laid in the bed of love, when home they won.
> Yea, and Achilles' very heart was wrung
> With love's remorse to have slain a thing
> So sweet
> Who might have borne her home, his queenly bride,
> To Chariot-glorious Pythia; for she was
> Flawless, a very daughter of the Gods
> Divinely tall, and most divinely fair.[14]

Achilles is said to have thrown himself on Penthesileia's corpse, weeping for having killed instead of courted her.

This theme of the Amazonian experience—of the strong woman who is vanquished by a man through treachery or deception—is also found in the myth of Atalanta.[15] Having beaten Peleus in a wrestling match, Atalanta was acknowledged as the strongest mortal, man or woman, in the ancient world. She always hunted with men, and it was she who stood ground at the onrush of the Calydonian boar and dropped him with an arrow as her male companions scattered for safety. But it was for her speed afoot that Atalanta was especially famous. She offered to marry the man who could beat her in running, but the penalty for losing was stiff. The heads of unsuccessful suitors lined both sides of the track.

Melanion, not wanting to lose his head over Atalanta permanently, hit on the scheme of rolling apples to her side as she raced. (Another version of the myth says that Aphrodite intervened on Melanion's behalf to toss out the apples; in any case, they were symbols of sexual love.) Unable to resist stopping to pick up the apples, Atalanta lost the race and married Melanion. Their marriage ended disastrously when Zeus, jealous as usual, turned them into a pair of lions.

And in medieval Europe, a similar story served as the basis of the Niebelungenlied legend from which Wagner wrote his Ring Cycle. Brunhild is deceived by Gunther, who gets his stronger friend Siegfried to impersonate him in a wrestling match with the queen. After she yields to the impostor, Gunther takes his place and the marriage is consummated; Brunhild never knows that she's been duped. In the Scandinavian version of the same story, the queen dies; her death is represented as a noble sacrifice. To the tune of some of the most beautiful music every written, we get the message that strong women must be put down by any means; that it may be good for them to suffer and die. (It was, of course, this version of the legend that Freud knew.)

The only legendary occasion on which a man conquers a woman through superior endurance, without hurting her, is the myth of Achilles' parents—the goddess Thetis, one of the fifty seagoing Nereids, who were all expert swimmers, and the mortal wrestling champion Peleus, whom later tradition recalled as the most outstanding of all Greek men.

At first Peleus tried to win Thetis with flattery, presents, and prayers, but the goddess wasn't interested. Next he surprised Thetis as she slept on the beach, and tried to take her by force. But he had forgotten that immortality bestows certain tactical advantages, and Thetis became in turn a lion, a snake, a bird, a tree, and finally a succession of horrible monsters which sprayed Peleus with fire, water, and ink.

Proteus, a prophetic sea god and, like Thetis, a quick-change artist, advised Peleus that the only way to win the goddess was to wrestle with her again—and just hold on. This Peleus did, enduring another soaking with water and ink and getting burned, mauled, and stung. But through sheer endurance he was finally able to overcome her with a hold from which she could not escape. Taking the form of a tender fish, Thetis says, "Some god is on your side, I yield. See Thetis in her proper shape revealed."

The Peleus-Thetis encounter seems to symbolize the struggle between the goddess-worshipping matriarchy and the new patriarchy—and to propose an ideal solution: that women should be able to express themselves fully, and that a man under no circumstances should hurt a woman.

Another symbol of the ancient feminine ideal was Cyrene, who, like Atalanta, was famous for her speed afoot. The sixth-century poet Pindar called her the "fair-armed daughter of Hypseus, who cared not for merry banquets with stay-at-home maidens of her own age" and preferred instead to work in the fields and protect the flocks with her father. Other myths say that the king of Libya promised part of his kingdom to the person who would slay a lion that had been ravaging the countryside. Cyrene killed the lion and was rewarded with the tract of land. Among the sculptures of Cyrene's exploits is a relief at the British Museum that shows her strangling a lion and on which is inscribed:

Cyrene, Mother of Cities,

Slayer of Lions, in token of great hospitality.

Impressed with Cyrene's tremendous strength and vitality, Apollo, said Pindar, wanted her for his bride.

In the several centuries before the birth of Christ, figures of Penthesileia, Atalanta, Thetis, and Cyrene were portrayed on household articles and common items as universal symbols of courage and strength. On the armor of Roman soldiers as well as on women's mirrors, on candelabra, storage cases, and burial vaults, these mythical heroines kept alive the positive view of women through several centuries after Christ.

Unfortunately, this Amazonian ideal was never fully realized, as the tragedy of Achilles and Penthesileia attests. Upon Penthesileia's death, the Amazons ceased to be a major threat to Greek society. Herodotus writes the finale, which began when a Greek army captured the last of the Amazons at the Thermadon River. The prisoners were loaded aboard three ships, he says, which weighed anchor and headed back toward the mainland. But the women made a last stand, rebelled, and massacred every man on board. Taking over the ships, they sailed off to Asia Minor, went ashore and, according to one account by Diodorus, got into trouble rustling horses.

Annoyed by the behavior of the invaders and entranced by their appearance, the Scythians, who had only recently invaded Asia Minor themselves, decided to make friends. They sent their youngest, best-looking men to the Amazon camp with instructions to be friendly and avoid combat. When the Amazons understood the men's intentions, they agreed to accept them as lovers and husbands in exchange for the right to continue riding, hunting, and using bows and javelins. (Communication must have been difficult because of the language barrier, and Diodorus says they all used sign language. Eventually the Amazons learned the Scythian tongue, but the men never mastered theirs.)

It has recently been established that the Scythians inhabited the vast plains that stretch from southern Asia Minor to the Orient, and made periodic forays into the Mesopotamian and Mediterranean regions.[15] The area they occupied is now part of southern Russia, which suggests that some modern Russians might be direct descendants of the ancient Amazons.

When this theory was suggested in a letter to famed geneticist Curt Stern in 1964, he replied: "It is indeed genetically possible that genes determining physical characteristics could have been passed from the ancient Amazon women in the course of centuries into the women of modern Russia. Indeed, such genes would have been transmitted into both men and women. As to the interbreeding of the Amazons and Scythians . . . If there is such evidence then one can say that any intermixture that has occurred once will be retained indefinitely."

Today Russian women athletes are discriminated against for the same reasons the Amazons were. The public image of a Russian female track and field star is of a big, burly, "masculine" woman—an image that sports-page editors perpetuate because it conforms to popular stereotypes. Of course there *are* burly, overweight athletes, in all countries and of both sexes. But in Russia, as elsewhere, the majority of female athletes are physically attractive. (Earl Taraldsen, former U.S. Olympic athlete and later an official at the games, said that

Russian women gymnasts were among the most beautiful women he has ever seen. Anyone who watched the 1972 Olympics would probably agree.)

If today's Amazons are hiding behind the Iron Curtain, women of the free world can console themselves with memories of the day when Hippolyte's daughter was on their side. In 1941, the Amazons enjoyed a brief, two-dimensional renaissance in American newspapers and comic books in the person of Wonder Woman. According to the cover description, she was "as lovely as Aphrodite, as wise as Athena—with the strength of Hercules." Created by the late psychologist William Marston, Wonder Woman was the only daughter of Hippolyte to whom Athena's spirit appeared: "American liberty and freedom must be perserved," said Athena. "You must send your strongest and wisest Amazon—the finest of your wonder women, for America, the last citadel of Democracy and of equal rights for women, needs your help."

Wonder Woman flew over from a place called Paradise Island to spend the war years in America and headed home again soon after Marston died and World War II ended. (The comic strip passed into other hands, then faltered and eventually failed.) After the men came marching home, America ceased being a "citadel for equal rights." It was back to Dagwood and Blondie and postwar domesticity.

So yes, Virginia, there really were Amazons. They were strong, courageous, kind, and superb athletes—particularly on horseback. And they symbolized the status of women in the earlier Silver Age, when women "led a free, natural and largely open-air life," as historian Charles Seltman has noted, "in which respect their habits contrasted markedly with various later historic periods."

In the Egyptian Old Kingdom (c. 1400 B.C.), Seltman

writes in his book *Women in Antiquity,* women owned their own houses, fields, and other property "to such an extent that in some circumstances the husband was little better than a lodger."[17] During the "Silver Age," women—probably Amazons—established and governed several cities, including Ephesus, Smyrna, Cyme, and Myrine in Asia Minor. In Mycenaean Athens as well as in Crete, women competed with men in athletic contests. One ancient Cretan monument portrays a bullfight in which a woman acrobat holds a bull's horns while a man catapults across the animal's back to be caught by a female acrobat on the other side. Another scene shows a woman standing atop a bull.

What was acceptable for women in ancient Minoa is condered radical in modern Spain, where Angela Hernandez, a twenty-three-year-old *torrera,* is challenging an ancient law that prohibits women from fighting bulls on the ground. For some reason, women are allowed to fight from horseback, which Hernandez already does—has done, in fact, since the age of nine. But she would like to get her feet on the ground, she told reporters, for the same reason Willie Sutton said he liked to rob banks: "Because that's where the money is."

Hernandez's bosses are being bullheaded about the issue. "I'm all for women having equal rights," said Bullfight Association president Paco Camino. "But I repeat, women shouldn't fight bulls because a bullfighter is and should be a man."[18] Nevertheless, women finally won their right in July 1973.

The athletic freedom enjoyed by Egyptian, Minoan, and Mycenean women was carried through the eighth and seventh centuries in the Spartan culture. Spartan society has gotten a bad name, undeservedly so in the opinion of historian Seltman, because of Athenian philosophers and historians who were "quite unfriendly to the culture." The

127

Spartans, he asserts, were not nearly so brutal as some fifth-century historians would have us believe. (Athenian writings were no doubt colored by the fact that Sparta had just defeated Athens in the Peloponnesian wars.) "No women in history have led such well-adjusted lives as the women of Sparta," Seltman believes.

The goals of Spartan society were chauvinistic, but within the warrior state, women were almost totally free. In order to bear strong sons it was understood that women had to be strong, resolute, and brave. The Spartans encouraged intensive physical training for women. From early childhood the women engaged in gymnastic exercises, and when they reached adolescence they entered into contests with each other—and often with men—in wrestling, racing, and throwing the quoit and javelin.

The Spartan idea of keeping women fit for motherhood was a switch on the matriarchal practice of selective breeding for strength. The late psychiatrist Karen Horney, along with a number of anthropologists, has theorized that the modern male's greater strength is the result of female selectivity in the distant past. According to Edward Carpenter, "the males in ancient times have been selected by the females on account of their prowess, superior strength or beauty; and this led to the evolution of a type which was the ideal of the female. But when, in the later history of mankind, property love set in, this action ceased. Women then became 'property' and man began to select women for the characteristics that were pleasing to him, and consequently the quality of the whole race began to be affected."[19]

There are ancient precedents to the notion that women should select suitors through physical challenge, choosing a man only if he showed superior strength and endurance. In *The First Sex*, Elizabeth Gould Davis reports that a variation on the Atalanta legend was still current as recently as 1908 in Siberia, where "it was reported of the Koryak that the suitor who could not overtake his beloved in a foot race was rejected by her."[20] And in Malaysia during the nineteenth century, a similar test was traditional. A bride would run into the forest with the groom in pursuit; if he was outrun, the wedding was off.

Simone de Beauvoir believes that the subjugation of women arises from a masculine will to perpetuate the family and hold on to property. Should, however, a society arise in which there is no idea of family, women achieve almost complete liberty and considerable power. Sparta was such a society, as were most of the cultures of the Silver Age.

"Owing to the wastage of man-power," Seltman writes in *Women in Antiquity*, "it came about that by the Hellenistic Age, some two-thirds of the land in the Lacedaemonian State was owned by women. The power which this gave them was remarkable." And he adds: "Yet they never used [this power] to attempt to change the hard life of their men."[21]

Although Seltman draws no conclusions from this, one might speculate that the Spartan women had no good reason to change the warlike ways of their men and many good reasons not to. As long as the warriors were preoccupied with violence, they weren't around to usurp power and property.

Unfortunately for the future of women, Sparta's military victory over Athens was followed by philosophical defeat. Athenians deplored the "vulgar" Spartan emphasis on physical fitness and professed shock at the Spartan habit of exercising in the nude. (Or almost nude—Spartan girls wore little sleeveless shifts called *peploi.*)

"Wish as you might," Euripides said in *Andromache*, "a Spartan girl never could be virtuous. They gad abroad with young men with naked thighs. And with clothes discarded, they race with 'em, wrestle with 'em. Intolerable!"[22]

Spartan women were not, in fact, what we would today call promiscuous. Temporary love affairs were accepted by men of the period as normal. "The husbands were somehow freed from any passion of jealous possessiveness of their wives," writes Seltman, "because it was held honorable for a free Spartan to share with any of his equals in the begetting of children. A middle-aged man with a young wife would introduce a younger man of good presence and breeding to his wife, and, if the wife approved and was pleased with him, the older man would happily accept as his own the offspring of such a temporary union. . . . Furthermore, such was the social freedom enjoyed by the married women, who even as children inherited estates on an equal footing with their brothers, that they were frequently able to run two households with a separate husband for each. Strangely enough, only one case is recorded by the historians of a man running two households, and therefore having two wives."[23]

The Spartan women's enviable position didn't last long. There were some men in Athens who weren't out on the battlefield, who instead of fighting spent most of their time thinking. The men had names like Xenophon and Aristotle, and they were among the first of a new breed of scholars who sought to explain and justify human behavior through the application of logic.

One of the things the new philosophers spent a lot of time explaining and justifying was the patriarchal system. If men were to be dominant, they had to have *reasons* to be; and so the philosophers came up with some. Sweeping away all empirical evidence to the contrary, they created, through deduction, different "natures" for each sex.

"For he [God] made man's body and mind more capable of enduring cold and heat and journeys and campaigns and therefore imposed on him the outdoor tasks," Xenophon wrote. "To the woman, since he has made her body less capable of such endurance, I take it that God has assigned the indoor tasks."[24] And in one of his dialogues between Ischomachus and Socrates, Xenophon has the great philosopher ask, "How does the Queen Bee's task resemble that of a woman?" Answer: "She stays in the hive."

Aristotle was more specific: "The male is better conditioned and more fit in every function; the female sex has a more evil disposition than the male, is more forward and less courageous and less honest. . . . For females are weaker and colder in nature, and we must look upon the female character as being a sort of natural deficiency . . . a misbegotten male."[25]

Plato tried vainly to salvage the rights of women, arguing that both sexes were entitled to equal physical and intellectual education.[26] To men like Euripides, he suggested that clothes might be made a requirement for feminine participation in athletic competition. The real issue, of course, was not nudity but property—though prudery served as a good ploy.[27]

Plato's opposition shouted him down, and by the fourth century B.C. women had indeed become the passive, indoor sex. No woman was allowed to attend any athletic event in Greece, under penalty of death. The Olympiad, where women had once competed on an equal basis with men, now barred them even as spectators. Should a female dare to sneak into the Games, as mothers and wives of competitors were tempted to do, she was to be removed immediately and tossed off a high ceremonial rock on a cliff.

Alexander the Great was one of Aristotle's most apt pupils, and before long the image of weak, passive, and domesticated woman had spread through the Macedonian empire.

One of the results of downgrading women's physical image was the emergence of sexual practices that have persisted ever since. Homosexuality, which a millennium before Christ had been sporadic enough to be remarkable, became virtually the norm. So did prostitution, which had formerly existed only as a religious fertility rite with very different implications; and for centuries afterward, some of the most powerful women in the world were not property owners but mistresses. Christianity and other religions introduced yet a new alternative: abstinence. If women were mentally inferior and physically deficient, as the philosophers attested, then the only alternatives for men would be to exploit them, idolize other men, or do without sex altogether.

The ancient, unrestricted view of woman is reflected in some parts of the Old Testament, but her image changed long before the time of Christ. Consequently, the traditional Judeo-Christian ideal most churchgoers recognize reflects the Athenian-Aristotelian rather than the Hebrew-Christian philosophy.

Golden Age philosophy was incorporated into many church writings, where it virtually became law. Any new scientific idea or theory was subsequently judged not on its own merits but on the degree to which it conformed both to the writings and to ancient Greek philosophy. In the sixteenth century, for example, when Copernicus challenged the Ptolemaic notion of a fixed earth and finite universe, all Christendom broke loose. (Giordano Bruno was burned at the stake in 1600 for espousing such heretical ideas.)

The ideas of Copernicus eventually prevailed, putting the physical sciences on the right track. But the social sciences, which evolved centuries later, based many of their theories on the old Aristotelian premises. You might say that women are still waiting for their Copernican revolution (which celebrated its five hundredth anniversary in 1973).

As the Aristotelian view of women became more and more entrenched, the parts of the Bible that referred to the earlier image of woman—to her physical strength and intellectual equality—were ignored by scholars and interpreters. Perhaps the best example of this is the poem that concludes the book of Proverbs (31:10), so often quoted at Mother's Day sermons as the description of the "ideal" wife. She not only rises early in the morning to care for her family, she makes clothes for them all, as well as the cloth from which the garments are made: "She lays her hands to the spindle and her hands hold the distaff."

Those verses from the passage that are almost never quoted, however, give rather a different picture of this woman: "She makes fine linen and sells it; and delivers girdles to the merchant. . . . She considers a field and buys it; with the fruit of her hands, she plants a vineyard." Or: "She girds her loins with strength and strengthens her arms." Modern commentaries omit explanation of this passage. And when James Michener used a translation of Proverbs 31 in his novel *The Source,* he left it out entirely.

The verse refers to the ancient practice of girding up tightly for any great exertion with a belt of fabric or leather worn across the chest and loins. A man who was seen either without his girdle or "loosely girded" was considered effeminate in those days. To be "ungirt," in fact, became an expression of unmanly indulgence.[28] But women, according to modern interpreters of the Bible, aren't supposed to be girt at all. (Unless, one assumes, it's by Playtex.)

Church fathers of the second, third, and succeeding centuries A.D. continued to stigmatize woman as a necessary evil, using terms reminiscent of Aristotle. For Tertullian, woman was "the mother of all human ills". For St. John Chrysostom she was a "natural temptation, a desirable calamity, a deadly fascination, and a painted ill." Later, both St. Augustine and St. Thomas Aquinas agreed with Aristotle's definitions, stating that woman's exclusive function was procreative.

By the sixteenth century, Martin Luther was excoriating women with the same vehemence he usually reserved for the Pope. "If woman grows weary and at last dies from childbearing, it matters not," he ranted. "Let her only die from bearing. She is there to do it." John Knox nourished similar sentiments: "Nature I say doth paint them further to be weak, frail, impatient, feeble, and foolish."

The Swiss physician Paracelsus, a contemporary of Luther who did for medicine what Luther had done for religion, gave lip service to the Judeo-Christian ideal of male and female unity expressed in Genesis 1–2. "God created man directly from the matrix. He took him from the matrix and made a man of him. . . . And then He gave him a matrix of his own—woman . . . to the end that henceforth there may be two of them, and yet only one; the two kinds of flesh, and yet only one, not two. This means that neither of them is perfect alone, that only both together are the whole man. . . ."

But after this auspicious beginning, Paracelsus proceeds to swallow Aristotle whole:

"Even though the female body was taken from the male, it cannot be compared to it. It is true that in shape it is similar to the male body, for woman too is formed as a human being, and like man she carries God's image in her. But in everything else, in its essence, properties, nature, and peculiarities, it is completely different from the male body."[29]

Paracelsus's first statement helped to counteract some of the rampant misogyny carried on during the Renaissance in Aristotle's name. But his second statement helped to entrench the worst aspects of the old philosophy even more deeply into the foundations of Western civilization. Through him sexual differentiation came into the practice of medicine and ultimately into psychiatry.

Women didn't have a chance. First the father of science defined their nature for them and limited their roles. Then the church and the medical establishment enforced these limitations. By the nineteenth century philosophers, historians, educators, and biologists had two millennia of precedents to quote authoritatively. Any dissent was met with a variation on the one-hundred-million-Frenchmen-can't-be-wrong argument: all these wise men have been denigrating women for centuries, so they must be right.

And by that time most women were so oppressed that they literally couldn't put their frustration into words. (After all, they weren't allowed to go to school.) Having come to believe that they were indeed frail, they took to venting their feelings in fits of fainting and hysteria. Most of them played the femininity game. Those who didn't began tentatively to demand equal rights—marching, singing, and getting thrown into jail.

And then a brand-new science came along, coining impressive new words with suffixes like *osis, enia,* and *oid.* The gentleman who founded this new science took all the old Aristotelian arguments, added a few more recent variations, wrapped them all up in dense Victorian prose, and pronounced that any woman who didn't conform to the theories was, well, mad.

9

THE PSYCHOLOGICAL BIAS

By the end of the nineteenth and throughout the
twentieth century, the portraits of madness executed
by both psychiatrists and novelists were primarily
of women.

Phyllis Chesler
Women and Madness

Sending a woman to a Freudian analyst is like sending a Jew to a Nazi.

Gloria Steinem

For centuries, women's bodies had been overworked in the
lower classes, corseted in the upper, raped and beaten and
often burned, regardless of class. Now their *minds* were
analyzed and defined—in terms of their abused bodies.
Anatomy was said to be their destiny: an inferior destiny,
the new scientists reasoned, because their bodies were so
obviously inferior—though well designed for the convenience of man and the bearing and nurturing of children.

Until Sigmund Freud arrived with his psychoanalytical
reinforcements, men were slowly on the retreat in the battle
for equal rights in some important areas. Higher education
had not only become open to women but, in some institu-

tions, open exclusively to them. Armed with new knowledge and confidence, they were demanding the right to property and suffrage.

But the science of psychiatry outflanked them with what was heralded as even newer knowledge—backed up by impressive empirical evidence and theoretical precedent. The analysts, in the tradition of the logicians and theologians who preceded them, saw the feminists as sexual misfits who could hardly speak for other women, since they weren't "normal" women themselves.

All of it was, of course, a rewrite of the same old script, casting women in the same old roles. But the reviews were terrific. And this time, should women fail to take their cues, they were dismissed from the social theater with a dishonorable diagnosis and sent to their new directors for coaching.

Freud had first redefined the rules of the femininity game, then supported his theories with case histories of women who had gotten sick playing it. As Shulamith Firestone has written, "Freud was merely a diagnostician for what feminism purports to cure."

The type of woman central casting was looking for, then as now, was physically passive, dependent, narcissistic, nonaggressive, and noncompetitive. The defiant, independent suffragettes were pronounced "neurotic"—emotionally arrested victims of something called "penis envy." (At least Freud didn't say they were "misbegotten men.")

"[Women] refuse to accept the fact of being castrated and have the hope of someday obtaining a penis in spite of everything," Freud wrote. "We must not allow ourselves to be deflected from such conclusions by the denial of the feminists, who are anxious to force us to regard the sexes as completely equal in position and worth."[1]

In terms of chromosomes, as we've seen, men are really

incomplete women. But genetics was in its infancy when Freud was writing (Mendel had begun his investigations in the mid-nineteenth century, but no one paid attention to his theories until thirty years after his death), and Freud focused on visible rather than microscopic differences between the sexes. And the most obvious of these was genital.

In infancy, Freud decided, little girls must be traumatized by the discovery that they lack a phallus. All the emotions, attitudes, and character traits we think of as feminine must, he reasoned, be reactions to this trauma. Only through bearing children could a woman compensate for her deficiency (giving birth, as it were, to substitute penises).

Today it seems incredible that anyone could take such an idea seriously. There are all sorts of male prerogatives that adult women might envy; the penis, except insofar as it is a biological passport to freedom, is not among them. Little girls may be intrigued by the penis, may feel envy when they first discover they don't have one, but the theoretical ramifications that have been drawn from this are ridiculous.

A few analysts and all leading feminists have attacked the penis-envy theory, but their opinions haven't made much of a dent in the professional picture. *Noyes' Modern Clinical Psychiatry*, a standard medical-school text (1968 edition), notes that "the girl may become aware that she has no penis and believes she had one but lost it, with the result that she develops feelings of inferiority and jealousy." In 1964, Eric Berne said that penis envy was the dynamics behind the marital game he called Frigid Woman. And any woman who has been to a psychiatrist recently is likely to have found the phallic pillar of Freudian theory still erect.

In fact, most of the country's leading psychiatrists are

still faithful to the basic premise of Freud's psychology of woman—namely, a woman's behavior is to be interpreted in the limited physical terms of her genitalia and her womb. Listen to them:

Joseph Rheingold: "Anatomy decrees the life of a woman. . . . When women grow up without dread of their biological functions and without subversion by feminist doctrines and therefore enter upon motherhood with a sense of fulfillment and altruistic sentiment, we shall attain the goal of a good life and a secure world in which to live."[2]

Bruno Bettelheim: "As much as women want to be good scientists and engineers, they want, first and foremost, to be womanly companions of men and to be mothers."[3]

Erik Erikson: "Young women often ask whether they can 'have an identity' before they know whom they will marry and for whom they will make a home. Granted that something in the young woman's identity must keep itself open for the peculiarities of the man to be joined and the children to be brought up, I think that much of a woman's identity is already defined in her kind of attractiveness and in the selectivity of her search for the man (or men) by whom she wishes to be sought."[4]

Erikson goes on to say that men are outer-directed while women are preoccupied with "inner spaces." He bases this notion on the observation that preadolescent girls, asked to construct something from blocks, build rooms and houses —supposedly reflective of their uterine inner space. Little boys, on the other hand, prefer to build towers or tall buildings, reflecting you know what. It does not occur to Erikson that such differences—which, of course, have indeed been observed—are more reasonably explained by conditioning than by sexual equipment.

One wonders what Erikson would say about the exploits

in open cockpits of aviation pioneers like Jeannette Piccard, Jacqueline Cochrane, and Blanche Scott, who obviously preferred outer spaces. And he would have to concede that a traditional use of inner spaces doesn't preclude a mastery of outer. In the 1972 Women's Transcontinental Air Race (unfortunately nicknamed the Powder Puff Derby), the first three places were won by grandmothers, each of whom had four children and four grandchildren. There were also five mother-daughter teams included in the entries, as well as a great-grandmother who flew in the race for the first time. Kay Brick, a psychologist and former schoolteacher who heads the TAR's board of directors, says of inner spaces: "After flying, I couldn't stand to go inside a school building again. It's too confining."

The theories of Freud and his modern followers have had a devastating effect on woman's physical image. The Freudian's blueprint for femininity is primarily sexual, with activity confined to procreation and psyche defined in reproductive terms—passive, supportive, and seductive. As recently as 1969, these qualities were listed as ideal by a lecturer in an introductory psychiatry course at the Columbia University College of Physicians and Surgeons, who illustrated his lectures with films of young women displaying these traits.[5]

"Normal" women are supposed to derive satisfaction from the way in which their bodies conform to stereotype. They are expected to be preoccupied with their face, their hair, the softness of their skin. Tragically, many women who feel free to be proud of a "masculine" characteristic—their strength—are, as Phyllis Chesler has cited, among those hospitalized as schizophrenic.

"Female schizophrenics were significantly less sensitive to their 'feminine' appearance than were either normal females or male schizophrenics," she writes (adding that this lack of concern has dire consequences when these patients seek to be released from asylums). "In fact, female schizophrenics were more satisfied with their male or strength body parts than normal males were."[6]

Liberated by madness, women schizophrenics are apparently expressing feelings common to all young women, feelings that are repressed at maturity in the name of normality. Adult women are encouraged to turn their energy to erotic rather than athletic ends. Vigorous physicality or displays of strength are interpreted as indications of repressed sexuality, and sexual innuendo often accompanies any aggressive or competitive physical activities a woman enjoys.

Horses, for instance, are commonly viewed as phallic symbols—which ostensibly explains the young girl's passion for riding, abandoned in her late teens, presumably, when she confronts the real thing. A more sensible explanation might be that riding is one of the most acceptable and challenging forms of athletics open to girls and women, one which involves considerable skill and the control of another creature that has a mind and plenty of muscle of its own. Boys may wrestle with and subdue members of their own sex without reproach. Girls find that one of the few outlets for feminine aggressiveness is a horse.

Snide remarks about sublimation are also aimed at Long Island ladies who play tennis ferociously from dawn to dusk, at Essex County matrons who ride resolutely to hounds in inclement weather—the implication being that all these women need is a good screwing. In this vein one might also speculate that male fishing parties are essentially homosexual, the fish serving the same purpose for anglers that the horse supposedly does for girls. The motives of men in groups, of course, are not questioned. Their physical activities are an affirmation of machismo; women who behave that way are presumed to be sublimating their anatomical destiny.

Yet excess energy, after all, can be worked off in a variety of ways—from work to sex to sport. And surely it is not surprising that a woman whose husband spends more time at board meetings than in bed may find an afternoon on the tennis court or on a horse more invigorating than a liaison with a neighbor or a repairman.

In adolescence, boys have been found to be better adjusted emotionally and socially than girls because they have an athletic outlet for surplus energy, for the tension and anxiety created by social and school pressures. And, largely because of physical stereotypes that often belie their real feelings, women at maturity have more emotional problems than do men. As was noted in Chapter 2, women are far more likely to be neurotic, manic depressive, psychotic, or schizophrenic. Yet where can a woman go for psychiatric help without paying forty-five dollars for a forty-five-minute hour to have the stereotypes reinforced by a Freudian-oriented analyst?

According to the American Psychiatric Association, the problem is not pressing. "Patients just want to know whether a doctor is boarded and certified and to what association he belongs," said an assistant in the APA offices. "Theory doesn't matter, because most prospective patients don't know the difference."

For those who do know the difference, the directory of the APA won't offer much of a choice. As of 1972, virtually all psychiatrists and analysts registered with the association—some 25,000 in the U.S., Canada, and abroad—were orthodox or neo-Freudians. Representatives of other psychoanalytic theories, like those of Carl Jung, are "statistically insignificant," according to an association spokesman.

"It's hard to come by a Jungian analyst," added an executive in the APA's Washington office. "I think there's one out in San Francisco—Joe something-or-other—awfully nice guy, plays the banjo." He added that in twenty-five years of APA meetings he couldn't recall a single discussion of Jungian theory.

A subsequent check with the C. G. Jung Foundation for Analytical Psychology in Manhattan revealed that there are 107 registered Jungian analysts practicing in the United States (that makes approximately one for every 250 Freudians); and the majority of these are to be found in New York or San Francisco. (This doesn't include Jungian psychologists, for which there is apparently no separate registry.)

The proportion is lamentable, for Jung developed some theories that were potentially more relevant to feminine experience than any of Freud's.

Jung believed that each sex has within it the psychic vestiges of the other. The feminine element in all of us, he reasoned, is the anima; the masculine element, the animus. Only by recognizing and projecting the opposing sexual characteristics within ourselves on a member of the opposite sex and coming to terms with them can an individual become complete.

In other words, men must accept the feminine element in themselves by projecting the ideal upon a woman and accepting her, while women must recognize and project their innate masculinity (animus) upon a man. In doing this, said Jung, a person achieves psychic unity.

Implicit in what is really a mystical resolution of the conflicts created by artificial sex roles is the idea that because we are conditioned to stereotype, we project our real, hidden natures to the "appropriate" sexual figure. The trouble is that our stereotypes have become so plastic, so removed from reality, that we may have a hard time recognizing our animas and animuses beneath the Playmate's breasts or the Man from Marlboro Country's chest.

Jung was speaking only of psychological projections, but he recognized elsewhere that physique and psyche were in some way related. His own conditioning, admittedly, prevented him from seeing the physical significance of the anima-animus confrontation, and he was consequently conventional about the feminine role.

Nevertheless, Jung's recognition of the importance of "archetypes" (the mythical characters and symbols which are common, he believed, in our racial memories, our collective subconscious) has new significance today when the ancient history of woman is being analyzed and reinterpreted.

Perhaps if Jung were writing today he would see the archetypal importance of such myths as Achilles and Penthesileia, of Peleus and Thetis, of Atalanta and Melanion, and of Cyrene and Apollo. But unfortunately, though both Jung and Freud thought mythology important (Freud described it as "psychology projected on the external world"), they largely ignored or misinterpreted those legends that spoke of ancient conflict between the sexes.[7] What we got instead was Oedipus.

Oedipus is interesting, though hardly a universal archetype except insofar as he reflects ancient taboos against incest. Anthropologists have been unable to find evidence of Oedipal complexes among boys in many primitive cultures. And when you think about it, its application to our culture is a bit far-fetched. Oedipus was middle-aged when he met his father, didn't recognize him, and didn't know his mother was his mother until after he married her. But it's a catchy complex nonetheless and generally accepted as "a basically correct psychological feature of our own culture," according to *Noyes' Modern Clinical Psychiatry*. "Some suggest that the Oedipus reaction is determined by the behavior of the parents, not the child. It is certainly frequently true that fathers are more severe with their sons and more indulgent with their daughters. That mothers frequently reverse this relationship is constantly observed by psychiatrists. . . . In either case, the rivalry and hostility associated with the Oedipus reaction would follow quite naturally."[8]

Oedipus, you might say, was a victim of the femininity game. In a society where women are restricted to playing the game, mothers tend to live vicariously through their sons, burdening them with their own unrealized hopes. A great many fathers, weaned on the masculinity rite, are too frequently harsh and critical of their sons; others become losers in society's eyes, alcoholics, or Milquetoasts. Faced with masculine criticism, or the absence of a masculine figure, a boy will naturally cling to his mother until he reaches an age where this is considered sissified. Then he may overreact, feeling guilt in his warm attachment to his mother and resenting her for perpetuating it. He may hate his father for being too critical or for not living up to his masculine role.

If Freud had read the other myths, he might have augmented the Oedipus complex with an Amazon complex, which could handily describe the reaction women have when they are deceived and hurt by men. Usually women deal with the resulting conflict in one of two unsatisfactory ways. They may become falsely compliant in order to win love (the femininity game), or they may become hostile and vindictive. (And with so many sons of Achilles running around, it's hard to find another alternative.)

146

A number of men would seem to suffer from an Achilles complex—believing, as did Achilles, that the only way to handle a strong, aggressive woman is to subdue her by force and/or deception.

Freud and his successors were content to support their theories about feminine physicality and behavior in large part with case histories of women who were sick of the game. Relatively few analysts of prominence have ever disputed Freud's conclusions. Although some post-Freudians—most notably Karen Horney, Erich Fromm, Wilhelm Reich, and Jung—have made significant departures from Freudian dogma, their voices haven't been strong enough to make many changes in analytic practice as a whole.[9] Others, like Eric Erikson—who recognizes, surprisingly, that "Behind man's insistence on masculine superiority, there is an age-old envy of women"—have seen flaws in Freudian theory but failed to draw logical conclusions from them. They return instead of the old Aristotelian notion of "different natures." (In Erikson's case, "inner spaces.")

Except for the late Dr. Abraham Maslow, no analyst has ever studied healthy, happy women to find out what the secret of their adjustment was. Maslow's early research was based on case histories of abnormal women (most of them from Brooklyn). He died before his later work—which, he said, yielded very different results—was published.

Wilhelm Reich, whom Phyllis Chesler describes as a feminist in theory, disagreed with Freud on many points, contending that neither sex could achieve mental health as long as women were oppressed. Reich was also concerned with the artificial divisions between mind and body; and, despite a preoccupation with orgasms and orgone boxes, he is refreshing to read on this score, if only because of his radical departures from traditional theory. Unfortunately,

Reich's nonconformity won him ostracism by most of his colleagues. In later life, after his trial, he went mad himself —a development which served to cast doubt on all of his valuable early work.

So we are still stuck with Freud—a strange choice as an authority on feminine behavior. His pioneering into the frontiers of the subconscious, however brilliant, surely represented in part an effort to unscramble himself. This he may have accomplished, but where women were concerned, he failed—both in reality and in theory. Freud was engaged to a woman for thirteen years, during which time his only sexual impulses were vented in written correspondence with his fiancée; and he had to be dragged to his own wedding. In his seventy-seventh year, after most of his ideas had passed from theory into dogma, the father of psychiatry admitted to his diary that he didn't understand women.

"What do women want?" he wrote. "Good God, what do they want?"

10

ACHILLES INCARNATE

> "A little bit of rape is good for a man's soul," announced Normal Mailer in a speech at the University of California at Berkeley. While Mailer waxed outrageous and his audience enthusiastically heckled, someone tossed a burning jockstrap on the stage and a prancing pair of gay liberationists got themselves busted. . . . Finally Mailer invited "all the feminists in the audience to please hiss." When a satisfying number obliged, he commented: "Obedient little bitches."
>
> *Time,* November 6, 1972

Psychiatry didn't succeed in erasing the archetypal image of woman from collective memory, but the new science did manage to distort the ancient history of sexual conflict and to use it as a justification for the status quo. Brutal physical encounters between the sexes, in which a woman was forcibly subdued by male strength, came to be viewed as "natural" masculine and feminine behavior. After all, men had been getting away with wife-beating and rape for centuries, and women had been putting up with it. Thus, reasoned the father of psychiatry (Germaine Greer has noted that it had no mother), such behavior must be normal.

Thereafter, brutality and helpless submission gained psychological respectability under the new names of sadism and masochism. Women were told that it was part of their nature to be hurt, and to enjoy it. People tend to be awed by opinions that wear the authoritative badge of science and scholarship, and so most women came to accept this strange view of themselves.

Given this carte blanche for physical cruelty, the modern Achilles has become not just a heel but often an enthusiastic sadist. He's glorified in movies, television, and on stage, idealized in poetry and song, and is the hero of countless novels—not all of which are by Harold Robbins or Norman Mailer. When Mailer stabbed his wife in the back at a cocktail party a few years ago (she had called him a faggot), no one seemed particularly disturbed. His literary reputation was enhanced, and his wife (who fortunately survived) did not press charges. Though presumably no analyst would condone such extreme behavior, it is a logical extension of Freudian "normality."

"The sadistic acts are identified with the role of the male, who is depicted as the cruel attacker who inflicts pain and injury," wrote analyst George Gero, M.D., in a 1962 article for *Psychoanalytic Quarterly*. "The masochistic destiny is viewed as the woman's lot: she endures the cruel attacks and finds pleasure in yielding and submission. Freud clearly stated that sadism and masochism must be assessed in the framework of the bisexual organization and that their definition is accountable for the different roles of the male and female . . . as Freud justly emphasized, 'Anatomy is Destiny.'"[1]

The sadomaso picture hasn't changed at all in the decade since Gero wrote. In fact, you can now see it in wide-screen Panavision in half the movies with an R or X rating. And rape itself has become an almost commonplace female fate, a sadistic canape to the real *pièce de résistance:* murder.

Mailer made murder machismo. Hitchcock, in two terrifying films, has made it the justifiable result of mother-induced misogynism. In both *Psycho* and *Frenzy* there is a subtle implication that the horrible acts are somehow justified by the early mothering experiences that led to psychopathy—and by the behavior of the victims, whether too seductive, too independent, or too aggressive.

In *Psycho,* the killer, played by Tony Perkins, comes off as a basically nice kid screwed up by his late and overprotective mom, whom he has stuffed for posterity and placed in her favorite rocking chair. And the victim—graphically hacked to death in a shower—is, after all, a naughty girl who has run off into the night with the office petty-cash box.

In the 1972 movie *Frenzy,* the featured female victim (there are several) is the proprietor of a lonely hearts bureau, an aggressive, successful businesswoman who has divorced her alcoholic and insolvent husband (portrayed as sympathetic and put upon) and then further humiliated him by giving him money when he asked for it. She is first raped, then strangled with a necktie by a man whom *New York Times* critic Vincent Canby describes as a "genial London fruit wholesaler." After a long sequence in which she gasps and struggles for life, a picture of the dead woman's distorted face is flashed on screen. "In one agonizing sequence," Canby wrote, "we are put into the position of cheering on (well, almost) the maniac."[2]

"One very strong aftereffect of such a film is to graphically remind a woman of her vulnerability," wrote Victoria Sullivan in a *New York Times* article about *Frenzy.* "There is a warning implicit in the film: you need a man to protect you.

You're too independent. Lock yourself in. Bolt the door.
Stay out of sight . . . a woman alone is an invitation . . . I
suspect that many women will leave the theater experiencing
the same confused but intense sense of outrage. Must we
go on seeing endless images of ourselves as victims . . .?"[3]

Slick sadism (and a malevolent but sympathetic sadist)
also dominates the critically acclaimed film *A Clockwork
Orange,* whose antihero and his gang roam the city and the
countryside beating, raping, and murdering women and
beating at least one old man to a pulp. Among their victims
is a woman sculptor with an aggressive, abrasive personality.
She's crushed to death when the hero drops a sculpture
of a giant penis on her face. (A number of women who
saw the film at different times report that men in the audience
laugh at this sequence.) In another scene, a woman is raped
while her husband, lying gagged on the floor, is kicked by
other gang members.

As in the middle ages, when wife-beating finally became
so prevalent that the church began to speak out against it,
psychiatrists and educators today have begun to deplore the
extremes of violence and sadism seen in the media. Yet the
groundwork for much of it was laid with the post-Freudian
image of man as sadistic and woman as passive and
anonymous, a breathing Barbie Doll (with inner spaces)
whose only purpose is adornment, seduction, and reproduction.

Prostitutes and nymphomaniacs represent extremes of
feminine passivity and masochism, and because they have
been encouraged to cultivate their masochism, quite normal
women fantasize about prostitution and impersonal sex.
Increasing numbers of them are beginning to turn fantasy
into reality. At the Woodstock festival, women fornicated

openly with men, apparently oblivious to the crowds around them. And group sex has become an increasingly popular way for husbands and wives to escape boredom—as well as any real relationship with each other.

Phyllis Chesler has recounted case histories of women who were encouraged by seductive psychiatrists to act out their prostitution fantasies:

We would start a session and then all of a sudden I would find him lying on the couch next to me. . . . I was paying for therapy and asked whether I should be, but very hesitantly. . . . We never really resolved it. . . . He treated me like a whore, just like my fantasies—and I guess it worked—sexually. Psychologically, it was tearing me apart.[4]

Women have continued to buy these notions about masochism and passivity because girls are conditioned to them from infancy—the penalty for aggressive displays being withdrawal of love. In maturity, a woman who is repeatedly hurt by men blames herself and turns the hostility toward the men who have mistreated her inward, thereby losing self-respect and reinforcing this early conditioning.

"The environment exerts an inhibiting influence as regards both her aggressions and her activity. . . . It is above all the aggressive components that are inhibited," writes Helene Deutsch in *The Psychology of Women*. "The social environment not only rejects them but also offers the woman's ego a kind of prize or bribe for renouncing them. . . . Has anyone ever seen a father romping with his little daughter in any manner except lovingly? Does he ever encourage her to competitive struggles?"[5]

This would seem to be a pretty damning appraisal of the whole conditioning process, a good description of the femininity game in which little girls are blackmailed by fathers, brothers, and boy friends into repressing their true instincts. But Deutsch interprets it all in orthodox Freudian terms. In renouncing aggressiveness, "the aggressive forces that are not actively spent must find an outlet, and they do this by endowing the passive state of being loved with a masochistic character. Earlier we have tried to explain feminine passivity on the basis of the anatomical difference between the sexes. The same . . . applies to feminine masochism."

Women are permitted to be aggressive about, say, housework. They speak of "wrestling" with dishes and laundry, of being "licked before they start," of how housework "gets me down." They take out hostility in verbal sarcasm, gossip, crying—and withdrawal of friendship.

But athletic aggressiveness is usually associated with sexuality or immaturity. If a woman wrestles with a man, she's being either seductive, dykey, or tomboyish. In a recent column, Abigail Van Buren warns her readers about this kind of behavior:

Dear Abby: My daughter is almost sixteen, and she is giving me a big headache. She has always been a good athlete. As far back as I can remember she has played with the boys. Baseball and football were her fun. She never played with dolls or cared for girls. The boys come around and she wrestles with them. Then they tell her their troubles about liking other girls. No one has ever asked her for a date, and I have bought her lovely feminine clothes, but no one asks her. What can I do?

A Mother's Heartache

Dear Mother: Tell your daughter that a girl who wrestles and boxes with the boys becomes "one of the boys" and forfeits her femininity. She should start now to build a feminine image, acquire a few girl friends, and leave the rough-housing to the fellows.

154

Helene Deutsch's approach is a little heavier: The reason little girls want to play with boys is to satisfy their latent masochism.

"Another form of the girl's activity consists in banding together with boys," she writes. "This is most likely to occur if she has brothers. It is fascinating to observe how easily the urge to boyish activity is transformed into a masochistic trend. The boys admit the girls to their games as an equal if she allows herself to be beaten from time to time and is willing to perform exhibitionistic and humiliating acts. There are desperate cries and tearful complaints; soon afterward the boyish masochist is consoled and again engages in the same games. . . . It might be thought that the little girl accepts suffering for the sake of gratifying her natural need for activity. *But this is not the case* [authors' italics]. Actually, she is already a little woman, in whom the active and masochistic ingredients are operating parallel to each other. . . ."[6]

One wonders how many girls and women who have been physically abused by men in play have been persuaded that they were subconsciously asking for it by displaying aggressiveness.

"On a personal gut-reaction level I suddenly want to retaliate," wrote Victoria Sullivan in the *New York Times* after seeing *Frenzy*. "I want to see films about men getting raped by women. . . . I want to see the camera linger on the look of terror in his eyes when he suddenly realizes that the woman is bigger, stronger, and far more brutal than he. I suspect that [such] films . . . may be sicker and more pernicious than your cheapie, humdrum porno flick, because they are slicker, more artistically compelling versions of sadomasochistic fantasies and because they leave me feeling more angry and more impotent simultaneously."[7]

155

Off screen, male brutality has become a national epidemic. Wife-beating, child-beating, and other "family quarrels" account for the majority of calls received by police stations across the country—some 80 per cent in urban areas.

"I never thought anything like this could happen in my home, in my community. And never, in my wildest imaginings, did I think it could happen to me." The woman speaking had been brutally beaten by her husband and subsequently hospitalized as a result of a quarrel. According to the reporter who interviewed her for an article in *Good Housekeeping* (October 1972, "Our Home Was a Battlefield"), she has many middle-class counterparts.

Outside the home, according to FBI statistics for 1972, forcible rape now accounts for 11 per cent of the nation's crimes. And women make the easiest target for muggers.

If a man insults another man or physically abuses him, he expects retaliation. But when a woman is insulted, she is expected to take it "like a lady"—and usually does. If she is mugged or raped, it is assumed that she will scream and plead for mercy rather than resist physically; if she does resist, her efforts are expected to be futile.

Consequently, women behave physically much like beta wolves, cringing and offering their neck symbolically to the alpha in the pack, acknowledging the leader's superiority and their own harmlessness. Women would, of course, feel much more secure and self-confident if they had the physical ability to meet an attack, whether psychological or physical, with what psychiatrists call an "appropriate response."

Judo is a good way to start. It may be learned not only for self-defense, but as a way of acquiring a realistic sense of physical competence. Many women who take up the sport have a history of hostile encounters with brothers, older sisters, even parents. Judo offers a chance to work off hostilities, develop skill, and renew self-confidence.

"After two months at the dojo I am still in a state of temporary euphoria," Susan Brownmiller wrote in a recent *New York Times* op-ed article. "I can do a nasty wrist lock on any male partner who'll let me. I can even execute a passable hip throw if I'm grabbed in just the right places. I doubt if a mugger or potential rapist will be as cooperative, but I have just begun to fight. . . . Up against the wall, femininity. I've seen through your ruse. I'm going to be a street-fighting woman."[8]

And if one is forced to use it for self-defense, judo is an excellent weapon for a woman trained in the martial arts. Recently a judo school in New Jersey sent a questionnaire to several thousand women graduates, asking them if they had ever used the sport in self-defense. Of the 130 women who replied affirmatively, *all* said they had experienced no difficulty in fending off their assailants.

Some girls and women are strong enough to defend themselves without the assistance of judo training. A former North American roller skating champion (who didn't want her name used because she finds her physical strength embarrassing) reports that she can beat all four of her older brothers in either boxing or wrestling. And a New York high school girl tells how a boy she had defeated in eight consecutive games of ping-pong lured her onto a beach to wrestle with her and get even. "I fooled him. I got him down, and he couldn't get up."

These are not isolated examples. Beneath their supposedly frail exteriors many women potentially have more physical self-confidence than anyone might expect. And if more of them engaged in *playful* physical encounters with men, they might well be surprised to find out how strong they really are.

One young woman athlete—a superb swimmer and national kayak champion who had never competed with a man in a contact sport—became so intrigued with the idea that she went into the men's gym at the University of Michigan, found a wrestler working out who was approximately her size and weight, and challenged him on the spot. "I was just as strong as he was," she said later. "The only reason he beat me was that he knew a lot of holds and I had never wrestled before."

A newspaper editor recalls discussing the benefits of judo and wrestling for women at a party, whereupon a hefty male guest challenged her to try and throw him over her shoulder. "He must have weighed 250 pounds," she said. "I'm five eight and weigh 135, but over he went. It was tremendously exhilarating, particularly so when I walked over to another friend—a guy who was about six three—and said, 'You're next,' and he backed away."

Married couples have reported working out arguments on a wrestling mat, thereby saving days of verbal feuding and smoldering resentment. And the Atalanta tradition—the ancient concept that a man is not suited to a woman unless he can honestly beat her in a physical contest—has been revived by a number of young women.

"One day my fiancé and I got to fooling around and wrestling," said one California girl. "I got the feeling he didn't like how well I was doing. I was giving him a hard time, and he started to hurt me. That made me mad, so I pinned him down. He broke our engagement. I'm just glad it happened before we got married."

Most men are conditioned to put women down physically, to take their own physical superiority for granted, and to be either patronizing or contemptuous of feminine displays of strength and skill. Professional discrimination against women certainly reflects this attitude—which may, in fact, be largely responsible for the discrimination.

"Why is it," asks model Sunny Griffin, "that most of the men I know feel they have to beat a woman at every game they play, and if you try to tussle and mess around with them in fun, they always hurt you and twist your arms until they feel like they're coming loose at the sockets?"

Griffin sees a direct relationship between this kind of physical reaction and the professional male bias she finds in the entertainment world. "Guys our own age can't accept the fact that we can make more money than they can. It kills them when they're making $20,000 a year and they know we're making $60,000. So one of us gets married, and what happens? The guy quits the job he has, decides he has to be independent too, and really ends up doing nothing. The attitude becomes 'I'll get a job when you quit yours.' It's the same old story—men making us weak so they can feel strong."

Fortunately, some men *don't* feel threatened by feminine strength. "Paul wouldn't think of hurting me or trying to slow me down—even though I knocked him out of the boat in the finals of the Canadian tilting championships," says Marilyn Richards of Toronto. "We do everything together— run a mile every day, take a long canoe trip every summer—and manage our business."

"Few couples enjoy fighting for fun as much as we do," says the husband of writer Ann DeSantis Kurkjian, adding: "I don't know whether there's any connection, but we're the only couple ever to win a Pulitzer prize."

Some women credit their capacity to cope with tragedy to their ability to assert themselves physically. A twenty-year-old woman whose husband died of cancer six months after the birth of their first child said, "I know how to win—and lose. Wrestling with my brother taught me how to fight."

Whether or not physical attitudes are the major cause of professional discrimination, as Sunny Griffin asserts, women will have more respect for themselves—and have more fun—when they develop physical competence and feel free to act aggressively.

"Yet remember," Orestes said to Electra, "in women too, dwells the spirit of battle."[9]

11

THE NAKED APE ARGUMENT

. . . the basic, primary function of woman is to mate for the purpose of reproduction. Everything else has been superimposed, and women deny this at their peril. No matter what kind of political, economic, or social setup we may have in the future nothing is going to change the biological facts. Kate Millett can claim that gender identity is imposed by society, not genes, till she's blue in the face, but this doesn't make it true, as several anthropologists and psychiatrists have recently remarked.

> Helen Lawrenson
> "The Feminine Mistake,"
> *Esquire,* January 1971

Since I was five years old I knew I wanted to be a boy. I liked to play ball, ride horseback, and shoot rifles. I couldn't have cared less about dolls. . . . I could never wear my hair long or wear high-heeled shoes. These are things I've always associated with being feminine. . . . Everyone has accepted my surgery very well, and I can deal with them much better now. Physically, it's a different life. I am accepted and can function as a male in society without being stomped to death. But emotionally there's no difference. I've always been a male, as far back as I can remember.

> "Robert," a transsexual
> who underwent surgery to
> become a man, quoted in
> the *New York Times,* November
> 20, 1972

By the twentieth century, the concept of male supremacy —both physical and intellectual—seemed virtually invincible, protected as it was by a mesh of interlocking theories which "proved" woman to be subordinate by defining her nature in terms of her reproductive equipment. First the philosophers had used logical conjurement to demarcate woman's place in the world, and then theologians threw the weight of God behind these theories. Later, medical men charted the anatomical differences between the sexes, and psychiatrists, looking over the charts, announced that Anatomy Is Destiny.

But the science of anthropology had the last word. Recently, many popular anthropologists have taken to decreeing that these logical, medical, and psychological theories about women are backed up by millions of years of prehistoric precedent. Woman's place, they say, has always been in the cave—stoking the fire, minding the kids, and being a desirable mate for the Mighty Hunter. The female body was designed for the femininity game, and any other behavior is "unnatural." For proof, they add, one need look no further than the hamadryas baboon, whose family structure is similar to ours.

Of course it's true that nothing short of surgery can change the biological fact that males impregnate and females conceive. But beyond that fact, it is neither logical, sensible, nor helpful to conclude, as have so many scholars, that our anatomy determines our behavior.

According to the best available evidence there are no physical instincts, no behavioral characteristics, that can be called exclusively masculine or feminine. Differences in physical structure, in hormonal balance, in chromosomal patterns, are not the primary determinants of behavior. The relentless conditioning of males and females to gender role from infancy is a primary determinant; nurture, not nature, is our guide.

This concept of sexual neutrality is frightening to many, as hysterical reactions like Helen Lawrenson's attest. For if we cannot place the responsibility for human destiny on God—or, more recently, on instinct—the weight of the world has nowhere to rest but on us. And it is painful to consider that we may have botched the job.

"Darwin and Bates can claim we're descended from apes until they're blue in the face," Lawrenson might have written during the Scopes monkey trial. "But this doesn't make it true, as some theologians have recently remarked."

Before Darwin, we could blame everything on God—a loftier scapegoat, certainly, than a gorilla. But we got over that stage rather quickly (it's been only forty-eight years since Clarence Darrow defended Scopes), and today we welcome the most unflattering comparisons with our primate ancestors, conceding to them responsibility not just for our physique but for our behavior.

"Instinct" has served as a convenient excuse for the mess the world is in, for greed, belligerence, and hatred. If we succeed in annihilating each other, we can blame our genetic predisposition to aggression and territoriality. And should men feel any guilt about treating the female half of humanity so miserably for so long, it may comfort them to learn from anthropologists that they're just behaving like big baboons.

Although some anthropologists—most notably Ashley Montagu and Margaret Mead—have tried to free the science from misogynist bias, they have been upstaged by male supremacists like Morris, Ardrey, Tiger, and Lorenz. Robert Ardrey informs us that sexual roles have been biologically reinforced for about seventy million years; that masculine and feminine "instincts" are ineradicably etched in the sands of time. At one point, he seems to be saying that modern woman, by agitating for equal rights, is forfeiting the bliss she knew eons ago, swinging through the trees.

"Modern woman lives in a feminine Utopia," he writes in a passage from *African Genesis* that reads like Esther Vilar. "She is educated. She has been freed of the dustmop cage. No social privilege is denied her. She has the vote, the bank account, and her entire family's destiny gripped in her beautifully manicured hands. Yet she is the unhappiest female that the primate world has ever seen, and the most treasured objective in her heart of hearts is the psychological castration of her husband and sons."

He later adds that "our studies of the female in primate societies have not yet reached a definitive level."[1]

Much of anthropological theory is still at that same non-definitive stage, as Elaine Morgan points out in her excellent and entertaining book *The Descent of Woman*. A lot of the "prehistoric evidence" used to rationalize our twentieth-century madness and reinforce our sexual roles is, in fact, theory. For instance, a crucial twelve-million-year period during the Pliocene, some twenty million years ago—a period when woman and man evolved from quadruped to biped, from hairy to naked ape—has yet to yield a single fossil. There is thus no evidence to explain what happened in that twelve-million-year drought, when the forests dried up and our ancestors had to abandon the withering trees for arid plains.

Dr. Desmond Morris has speculated that during this period women developed her modern form—fleshy buttocks and pendulous breasts, along with various erogenous zones—both for the convenience and stimulation of her mate, the aggressive Mighty Hunter, and to ensure that monogamy or "pair bonding" would work. After pairing off, says Morris, there had to be some way of guaranteeing that couples would be faithful to each other. "The simplest and most direct way of doing this," he writes, "was to make the shared activities of the pair more complicated and more rewarding. In other words, to make sex sexier."[2]

And that is why, Morris theorizes, naked apes began mating face to face instead of front to back. To make face-to-face sex more pleasurable and enticing, females developed alluring breasts. (Morris leaves one with the odd impression that our female ancestors somehow anticipated *Playboy* twenty million years ago and evolved accordingly.)

Morgan's theory makes a lot more sense. She first challenges the widely accepted notion that, during the Pliocene drought, our small-brained ancestors—surrounded by hungry predators who were faster and longer of tooth, in an environment lacking their customary diet and shelter—managed to defy the overwhelming odds and emerge full-blown as the naked apes of the Pleistocene. How could this have happened? Ms. Morgan asks. "Did she take a crash course in walking erect?" (Morgan refers to our primate ancestors in the feminine pronoun.) "Did she convince some male overnight that he must now be the breadwinner and back him up by agreeing to go hairless and thus constituting an even more vulnerable and conspicuous target for any passing carnivore? Did she turn into the naked ape?

"Of course, she did nothing of the kind," the author answers. "There simply wasn't time. In the circumstances, there was only one thing she could possibly turn into, and she promptly did it. She turned into a leopard's dinner."[3]

Morgan goes on to speculate that one group of hairy apes managed to survive this awful period: those who lived in the forests closest to the sea. Instead of going out to the plains to be devoured, this group of apes retreated into the water. And after millions of years of swimming around, they lost most of their hair (because it weighted them down), learned to stand upright (to keep their heads above water), and figured out how to use pebbles and other objects to crack the shells of mollusks and other edible sea creatures. When danger threatened, these apes learned to retreat into the water.

In this aquatic environment, says Morgan, pendulous breasts were more convenient for nursing infants—whether the mother was standing waist-deep in water or sitting on the beach. And while she was sitting on the beach, a sub-cutaneous layer of fat was helpful to pad the pelvic bones.

Morgan's arguments are as provocative as they are witty. But she has been criticized for lacking the proper credentials to argue such an important point—her Oxford doctorate was not in anthropology but in literature. Unable to disprove her theories, critics have retreated to the refuge of the mediocre: academic one-upmanship.

And so we continue to hear ourselves endlessly compared to baboon colonies and gaggles of greylag geese.

"Women start from exactly the wrong point of view," anthropologist Lionel Tiger says in *Men in Groups* (Tiger started the business about male "bonding"—group behavior that's supposed to be exclusively male). "Rather than starting from the notion that males and females are the same, they should start from the notion that they are different and have different life experiences."[4]

They do, of course, have different life experiences, but these experiences are less the product of innate differences than of childhood conditioning and expectations—conditioning perpetuated by "experts" like Tiger, Morris, and Ardrey.

Anthropologist Margaret Mead has noted that though

our own sex roles have many primitive parallels, we should not overlook cultures like the Tchambulian,[5] where men curl their hair and mind the children while the wives are out fishing. And Columbia University professor Alexander Alland argues that recent culture is far more persuasive than genes as a behavioral determinant. We don't have to look back seventy million years, he says, but only a few thousand to find precedents for current behavior.

Yale anthropology professor David Pilbeam backs him up. "It is overly simplistic in the extreme to believe that man behaves in strongly genetically deterministic ways," he wrote in a 1972 *New York Times Magazine* article, "when we know that apes and monkeys do not. Careful ethological work shows us that the primates closely related to us . . . get on quite amicably together under natural and undisturbed conditions. Learning plays a very significant part in the acquisition of their behavior. They are *not* highly aggressive, obsessively dominance-oriented, territorial creatures."[6]

Mistaken ideas about man's innate tendencies toward violent aggression have been promulgated, says Pilbeam, because ethologists have studied captive primates. And imprisoned animals behave very differently from those in the wild, as do imprisoned people.

Primates in the wild play as a way of releasing aggression and seldom resort to violence, engaging instead in "displays" to frighten opponents. Anthropologists have noted that sport is an acceptable way for man of all cultures to channel aggressive instincts. But in this culture women lack such a universal outlet, and feminine aggressiveness is vented verbally through gossip and sarcasm; emotionally, by crying.

Pilbeam goes on to attribute the sexual division of labor not to genetic or hormonal differences but to convenience: "The men in these [bush] societies hunt animals while the women gather plant food. However, women often scout for game, and in some groups they may also hunt smaller animals, while a man returning from a day's hunting will almost always gather vegetable food on his way. Thus the division of labor between sexes is not distinct and immutable; it seems to be functional, related to mobility. . . ."

The fact of female conception, of penetration by the male, has also been interpreted as a basic sign of feminine inferiority. Helen Lawrenson thinks she has Simone de Beauvoir backed up against the uterine wall on this point.

"Even Simone de Beauvoir, top-drawer member of the feminist hagiology, has written, 'the division of the sexes is a biological fact, not an event in history,'" writes Lawrenson. "After treating us to a survey of the sex habits of ants, termites (do you know that a termite queen lays up to 4000 eggs a day? Well, now you do),[7] and toads, she works her way up to birds, fishes, and mammals and admits that 'it is unquestionably the male who takes the female—she is *taken*. . . . The male deposits his semen, the female receives.'"

As to who gives and who takes, it all depends on your point of view—and your species. Female black widow spiders take their boy friends for all they're worth, biologically speaking, and then do them in. But we are not spiders, toads, termites—or even apes, any more. Our genitalia and genetic construction may be similar to that of many animals, but it hardly follows that this similarity causes similar *behavior*. In humans, for example, an extra Y chromosome in males, producing an XYY pattern, has been shown to result in violent and abnormal sexual behavior—with full fertility. In mice, the identical pattern produces a sterile but otherwise normal male.

"The mechanism of sex determination is very different

in different organisms," writes E. W. Caspari in *Sex and Behavior*. "It appears to be relatively easily modified in the course of evolution."[8]

But what about motherhood? Isn't nurturing an infant instinctive and exclusively feminine behavior? Doesn't it have to be instinctive among animals, so that the young will survive?

Part of the answer to this question can be found in the records of battered human infants admitted to hospital emergency wards, of newborns left on doorsteps and in garbage cans, or murdered by desperate mothers. As for wild animals, who said *they're* such great parents?

"Animals have to learn how to care for young too," says Dr. Heinz Meng, a zoologist and ornithologist at the State University of New York at New Paltz. "We have no way of knowing what the mortality rate of firstborns in the wild is, but I'd guess it is pretty high."

And in a recent letter to the *New York Times Magazine*, Dr. Rhoda K. Unger, a psychologist, wrote: "There is no evidence for hereditary, built-in urges toward nurturance of the infant among the higher primates. Harlow's work with monkeys has shown that females who have had little experience of such nurturance themselves show little interest in their own offspring." She adds: "There is a great deal of evidence that nurturant behavior is not limited to females. The ability to nurture in higher animals is neither an instinct nor limited to females. It must be learned and can be learned equally well by either sex. . . ."

Following comparisons with primates and other animals, hormones are the next most popular explanation of human behavior. Estrogen and androgen have been shown to trigger fear, anxiety, and aggressive tendencies, and it is suggested that testosterone, the male hormone, may "masculinize" the brain by organizing nerve centers in such a way as to cause men to respond differently to stimuli.

Hormonal activity during the menstrual cycle is said to explain violence in women as well as physical and mental illness. Some 49 per cent of female medical and surgical hospital admissions, the majority of psychiatric admissions, and 62 per cent of violent crimes committed by women occur just prior to or during the menses.

As recently as 1972, Dr. Edgar Berman, a retired surgeon and then a member of the Democratic Party's committee on national priorities, invoked hormones as a reason for keeping women out of politics. "Approximately half the people in this world spend much of their lives under the raging hormonal imbalance of the periodic lunar cycle," he said. "In middle age, they escape this monthly madness at last, only to enter a different but equally unreliable state, characterized by curious mental aberrations. In this demented condition they continue to plague the planet for another twenty-five or thirty years . . . their physical and psychological disabilities render them unfit to make important decisions or hold positions of power. The only job for which they are truly qualified is bearing of young."[9]

That's a frightening bias for a surgeon to have, and it's horrifying to speculate how many women have been permanently "cured" of their "raging imbalances" by Dr. Berman's scalpel. (Barbara Seaman has quoted a study in which one third of sixty cases of hysterectomy performed were shown to be unnecessary and another 10 per cent doubtful.)

Hormone levels, as was noted in an earlier chapter, vary greatly from individual to individual—regardless of sex. While studies about the influence of hormones on female behavior *seem* to show distinct differences between the sexes, they may also reflect the extraordinary behavioral effects of environment and upbringing. Women expect menstruation to change their mood (they've been conditioned to believe it from childhood), and they may take advantage of their periods to release all the anxiety and tension built up in the preceding days. They expect menopause to send them over the hill—as it in fact does in our society—and they may react hysterically.

If this seems like a feminist pipe dream, consider a study that was done at Johns Hopkins University on the origins of human sexual behavior—a study whose extraordinarily relevant results have been virtually ignored in the current debate on the subject.

Between 1955 and 1965, clinical psychologists at Johns Hopkins studied 113 hermaphrodites comprising all possible combinations of sexual characteristics. Each group included only individuals who had primary or secondary sexual characteristics or chromosome patterns *opposite* to those of the gender role in which they had been raised. In addition to the hermaphrodites, the researchers studied a group of girls with Turner's syndrome, a condition characterized by complete absence of the female hormone estrogen. (Unless estrogen is administered artificially, girls with Turner's syndrome fail to develop secondary sexual characteristics at puberty.)

All in all, the Johns Hopkins team had an ideal opportunity to determine whether role behavior is determined primarily by hormones and heredity or by environment.

The first group they studied comprised nineteen hermophrodites whose chromosome patterns contradicted their social gender role—in other words, those who had been raised as women had an XY pattern, and those raised as men had an XX pattern. "Without a single exception it was found that the gender role and orientation as man or woman, boy or girl, was in accordance with the assigned sex and rearing rather than in accord with chromosomal sex," wrote researcher Dr. John L. Hampson. "It seems to us, therefore, convincingly clear that gender role and orientation as male and female does not automatically correspond to chromosomal sex. Instead, it is in some way related to assigned sex and rearing." With the exception of five individuals, the same conclusions held for *all* other types of hermaphrodite studied.

As for the thirteen girls with Turner's syndrome, that study "is as dramatic as any experimental group one could devise," says Hampson. "These girls have no functioning gonadal tissue and undergo no somatic pubertal development unless they are treated with estrogens. The first nine patients were studied psychologically prior to substitution therapy. They were therefore totally lacking in any kind of ovarian hormone. Even so, every single one described daydreams and fantasies of romantic courtship, marriage, and sometimes of heterosexual erotic play which are indistinguishable from those of normal girls."[10]

John Money, one of Hampson's former colleagues in the hermaphrodite study, reaches similar conclusions in his 1973 book *Man and Woman, Boy and Girl.* According to Money, a medical psychologist, virtually all behavioral sex differences are culturally determined. He suggests that both sexes have the potential for behavior that has been thought exclusively masculine or feminine, such as violent aggressiveness and mothering—the only difference being a possibly higher threshold for releasing this behavior in the brains of each sex.[11]

At the December 1972 convention of the American Association for the Advancement of Science, Money cited a 1963 case in which a male infant's penis was accidentally severed with a cauterizing needle during circumcision. Physicians suggested that the parents transform the infant, through plastic surgery, into a girl. An artificial vagina was subsequently created and the child was raised as a girl. Today, at nine years of age, says Money, she is perfectly adjusted psychologically to "her" gender role.

Women's psychological problems are magnified because much of the behavior we consider "feminine" isn't strictly enforced until adolescence. And gender change in later life, says Hampson, causes severe psychological problems. Yet from the age of eighteen months to four years, a period which Hampson says is crucial in establishing gender role (synonymous with the development of language), many girls are allowed to display aggressive, tomboyish behavior which is later frowned on. In elementary school, as Margaret Mead has noted, girls and boys face each other "with the same stance, the same gleam in their eye."[12] It isn't until the adolescent years that different behavior is imposed and tomboys are expected to become "ladies."

Hampson concludes: "Psychologic sex or gender role appears to be learned. In place of a theory of innate constitutional psychologic bisexuality, we can substitute a concept of psychosexual neutrality in humans at birth."[13]

In brief, the most relevant evidence indicates that we are born neutral. It is our parents and their parents before them, our aunts, uncles, friends, and teachers who shape our roles. Even the tendency of a twelve-week-old female to gaze longer at photos of faces can be explained as a result of the more affectionate maternal handling that nearly all mothers give their daughters.

It seems reasonable to suggest further that rigid gender roles are responsible for much of what is called deviant behavior, both sexual and social. The definition of "deviant" varies directly with the definition of "normal." As long as women are locked into a gender role that defines as "normal" physical frailty and social passivity, those women who seek to break out of this role will be seen as deviates. As long as men are programmed to perform the masculinity rite, those who refuse to conform will be considered deviates, too.

Whether or not we can or want to rid ourselves of the concept of "normal" is moot. We might want to consider widening the concept, thereby making it possible for us to break out of rigid gender roles. When women and men begin to do this, both sexes will be in a much better position to function as full human beings.

12

ENDGAME

. . . And then Alice put down her flamingo and began an account of the game, feeling very glad she had someone to listen to her . . .

"I don't think they play at all fairly . . . and they all quarrel, so dreadfully one can't hear oneself speak—and they don't seem to have any rules in particular; at least if there are, nobody attends to them—and you've no idea how confusing it all is . . ."

"Who *are* you talking to?" said the king. . . .

"It's a friend of mine—a Cheshire Cat," said Alice. "Allow me to introduce it."

"I don't like the look of it at all," said the King. "However, it may kiss my hand, if it likes."

"I'd rather not," the cat remarked.

"Don't be impertinent," said the King, "and don't look at me like that."

"A cat may look at a king," said Alice. "I've read that in some book, but I don't remember where" . . .

The cat's head began fading away the moment he was gone, and, by the time he had come back with the Duchess it had entirely disappeared. So the King and the executioner ran wildly up and down looking for it, while the rest of the party went back to the game."

Lewis Carroll
*Alice's Adventures
in Wonderland*

Women today are justifiably as angry and confused as an Alice trying to win a croquet game against a demented

Duchess. The world they have finally awakened to is as mad as Wonderland; the rules given them to live by, even crazier. Under the circumstances, the mallet of equal opportunity is only slightly more useful than a flamingo.

For women have been set up to lose; conditioned against success by a combination of social pressure and ridicule, by medical, philosophical, and anthropological cant, by distorted history. Bribed with love and brainwashed by educators, they have sacrificed their identities and ambitions to become pawns in a rigged game.

The qualities necessary to success in today's culture—competitiveness, aggressiveness, the desire to achieve—are considered unwomanly, as is the game model for these qualities: competitive physical skill. Femininity is defined as passivity, as emotional dependence and physical weakness, as reaction instead of action; the portrait, in short, of a loser.

Even when a woman manages, somehow, to win a few preliminary bouts, she knows she will face a continuing fight against discriminatory handicaps that prevent her from competing equally. Just as career women still get paid less than men and are still unlikely to be promoted to positions of authority, sportswomen have to put up with inferior or nonexistent facilities, inadequate training, and regulations barring competition with their physical peers—when those peers are men.

And the approval, power, and self-determination that business success produces in men continues to be denied women. When women do work outside the home it is still, in so many cases, to supportively "help out" rather than to independently achieve personal success.

Finding that achievement brings more penalties than

rewards, most women give up—disillusioned, often exhausted—and retreat to the femininity game, where financial
security, power, and love can be gained through a man.

Wifehood and motherhood, roles that traditionally call
for selflessness and supportiveness, are still the only sure
guarantees of social approval and security. Passivity and
dependence being the traditional "feminine" traits of a wife
and mother, the institution of marriage provides a convenient
excuse for not acting, as well as a haven for those who have
tried to act and failed.

Over the long run, the femininity game is a losing proposition in which a woman sells her identity for love, or security,
or money—and relates, in the bargain, to other women as
potential competitors. But though the game has made many
women physically sick, mentally ill, habit-prone, self-conscious instead of confident, the penalties for success seem
worse: disapproval, insecurity, loneliness, and above all,
lovelessness. Not surprisingly, many find it less painful to
go on dreaming of princes and charting their crossed stars.

After three thousand years of conning and coercion—of
being victimized by their own illusions and by male delusions
—women find the prospects dim for making radical changes
in attitudes and images within a generation.

Right now, the most publicized remedies for the feminine
condition run to extremes. On one side are the antifeminists
like Midge Decter *(The New Chastity)*, Esther Vilar *(The
Manipulated Man)*, and Lucianne Goldberg and Jeannie Sakol
(Purr, Baby, Purr), who would persuade women that they've
never had it so good and/or are largely responsible for the
problems they are rebelling against.

Says Goldberg and Sakol, co-founders of something
called the Pussycat League: "Have our happiest moments

been the times we have outdone men, or have they been the moments we felt one with men, through affection . . . ? Do we want to create a society in which the only way you can tell men and women apart (if anyone cared) would be to check their I.D. cards? For us, the answer to all this is a resounding 'no' and a fervent plea to that great majority of women who rejoice in being women: 'Purr, baby, purr.'"

Says Vilar: "These are the reasons why women's liberation has failed: the enemies they fought were really friends, and the real enemy remained undetected [themselves] . . . their struggle was aided almost exclusively by men . . . the story of the underprivileged woman was an invention—and against an invention one cannot stage a rebellion. . . ."

The antimale radicals range from militants like Valerie Solanis, founder of SCUM (Society for Cutting Up Men), who set a precedent for feminine violence by shooting pop artist Andy Warhol full of bullets, to Dana Densmore, who is for life, liberty, and the pursuit of ugliness.

"You have to be prepared, then, to be not just unattractive but actually sexually repulsive to most men," Densmore says in "Sex Roles and Female Oppression," a widely circulated pamphlet. "If we are going to be liberated we must reject the false image that makes men love us, and this will make men cease to love us. . . . It will be a less friendly world, but there will be no unrequited longing. What we're really after is to be loved for ourselves, and if that's impossible, why should we care about love at all?"

The antifeminist point of view is a retreat; the antimale point of view mimics male violence and male exclusivity, and traps women in the reverse of the old sexual image. For whether women choose to be desirable or undesirable

178

to men, to love them or to try and destroy them, it is still men who are, so to speak, calling the shots.

But it seems like a waste of precious time and mental energy to promote either retreat or man-hating. Neither approach really qualifies as a plan of action, which is after all the name of the game women must now create.

Warlock-hunting, while diverting, accomplishes little for women and can have damaging side effects: the tendency, for instance, to view the winner's spoils and tactics—i.e., success, achievement, power—as masculine, per se, and to villify women who display or use them:

"If you are in the first category [an achiever,]" says Anselma del Olio in a book she is writing about her experiences in the movement, "you are immediately labeled a thrill-seeking opportunist, a ruthless mercenary, out to get her fame and fortune over the dead bodies of selfless sisters who have buried their abilities and sacrificed their ambitions for the greater glory of Feminism. Productivity seems to be the major crime—but if you have the misfortune of being outspoken and articulate, you are accused of being powermad, elitist, fascist, and finally, the worst epithet of all, a male-identifier . . . Arrggg!"[1]

The attitude she describes is really the same one that has kept women in "their place" for so long. No matter who's doing the name-calling, women still end up being supportive, modest, unsuccessful, and fearful of achievement.

Unfortunately it is easiest for everyone to think in terms of such opposites: winners vs. losers, egotistical vs. unselfish, masculine vs. feminine, oppressor vs. oppressed. Our authoritarian upbringing, our sexist conditioning compel us toward either/or choices. The extent of this compulsion was recently demonstrated by Stanford University psychologist Philip G. Zimbardo, who staged a six-day mock prison experiment to see how normal college students reacted when asked to play the role of guards and prisoners in a simulated environment. Three of the "prisoners" had mental breakdowns and had to be removed. The others became psychologically identical to real prisoners—first defiant, then passive, dependent, untrustworthy, disloyal to their mates, and obedient to the guards' whims. The guards, in turn, became physically sadistic and mentally cruel.

"The most disturbing implication of our research comes from the parallels between what occurred in that basement mock prison and daily experiences in our own lives—and we presume yours," wrote Zimbardo in an April 1973 issue of the *New York Times Magazine*. "The physical institution of prison is but a concrete and steel metaphor for the existence of a more pervasive, albeit less obvious, prison of the mind that all of us daily create, populate, and perpetuate. We speak here of the prisons of racism, sexism, despair, shyness, neurotic hangups, and the like. The social convention of marriage, as one example, becomes for many couples a state of imprisonment in which one partner agrees to be prisoner or guard, forcing or allowing the other to play the reciprocal role. . . . To what extent do we allow ourselves to become imprisoned by docilely accepting the roles others assign to us, or, indeed, choose to remain prisoners because being passive and dependent frees us from the need to act and be responsible for our actions?"

In the past, women have docilely accepted their feminine prisoner roles, and many men have acted like guards. Some women, given lenient guards, don't mind the status quo. But outside the boundaries of marriage, they tend to behave—or get treated—like ex-cons: finding their opportunities limited and their abilities rusty, they end up back behind bars. Others, once liberated, may be tempted to adopt the tactics of the guards.

Breaking out of behavior patterns like these, which confine the entire human race, will not be easy for women. But it is the only avenue of escape. Women must stop reacting and start creating new alternatives—not just for themselves but for men, for children, for the old, the minorities.

They will have to question, at the beginning, every moment of their behavior, every emotion, in order to separate real feelings from conditioned reflexes. Armed with the knowledge that the old roles are arbitrary creations designed to perpetuate the status quo, they must invent new attitudes and images.

What would such a "new" woman be like? Would, as Lucianne Goldberg and Jeannie Sakol suggest, her sexual identity be discernible only on an I.D. card? This seems unlikely, unless women suddenly take androgen shots, begin to speak in basso voices, and grow beards. Rather, the main change would be in a woman's new sense of self. Her behavior would not be limited by the expectations of others, nor would her appearance be a reflection of male fantasy. Once women have psychological control over their bodies they will be free to decide how to use them—whether to be mothers or long-distance runners or both. They will be free to pursue any goals without asking, before acting, whether a man would approve.

And when women begin creating options for themselves, the fears of diehard chauvinists and feminist reactionaries will probably prove unwarranted. The specter of test-tube babies, for one, seems unlikely to materialize. For if a woman chooses to be a mother, she will do so with pride in her physical ability to bear children. Should she decide against motherhood, she will feel no guilt, for her decision will not be based on the expectations of others.

One can also hope that woman's physical energy, which has for so long been channeled into seductive sexuality, would become attractive to other women, and appreciated by them. Until now, the physical appreciation that heterosexual men have always had for each other has been denied women who are not lesbians. In fact, the fear of being so labeled has caused women to shy away from the kind of physical camaraderie men enjoy. They have either envied each other's physicality or disparaged it. Acceptance of gay liberation within the feminist movement has helped to bring this hangup into the open. A new emphasis on athletic involvement and physical development should be equally influential.

Honest sexuality will perhaps be most difficult for the current generation of women to achieve, for sex is often seen now, by both men and women, as the finale of the femininity game. It is the ritual in which a woman loses—yields or submits—to the male and thereby wins love and security.

As long as sexual pleasure is measured on a scoreboard, women will continue to have sexual problems. And they will continue to be hurt by bedroom Achilleses if they persist in expecting love as a prize for "losing." This conflict hasn't been resolved within the new climate of sexual freedom, because woman's sexual image hasn't changed—it has just become more accessible and exploitable.

As women develop a greater sense of themselves and cease to function as a reflection of male fantasy, they will probably find themselves unable to be partners to impersonal sex, which necessarily degrades them. Women—and men— will be able to find greater excitement, love, and affection when the haze of role expectations is lifted. Certainly heterosexuality would be infinitely sexier if women felt free to challenge men at every level, and be challenged in return.

But if women are to create a new image and a new and more effective role in the world, they will have to use their justifiable anger to understand and act. Instead of defensively sniping at men and the establishment, they must offer a positive challenge to the status quo—they must transform themselves into winners.

What do women want to win, and how should they go about it? Because women are so relatively ineffectual politically, at the moment, their most immediate need is for power. Right now, men have a corner—a large corner—on it. There is nothing innately masculine about power, which in its basic, uncorrupted sense is simply the freedom to act, the ability to achieve, to control one's own destiny; and its misuse by men is no reason why women should shun it. As George Bernard Shaw wrote, "Power does not corrupt men, but fools who gain possession of power, often corrupt power."[2]

"Miracles of consciousness aside," Phyllis Chesler has written, "I see no way for women to defeat the rule of violence without achieving power. . . . To those who think I am suggesting that we have a war between the sexes, I say but we have always had one, and women have always lost it."[3]

To win the war—and end the femininity game—women will have to play, for the time being at least, a man's game; they will have to work realistically within (not *for*) the existing system. The rules may change to accommodate women; the structure must yield to reform; but the name of the game is likely to remain the same for generations to come.

This is not to say that women should imitate the more corrupt tactics of the masculinity rite nor conceive of victory in male terms. But they will have to work within the existing establishment until they are in a position to change it. To do so, they must cultivate the positive side of those qualities that have been denied them so long in the name of femininity. And, precisely because women have *not* been conditioned to the distorted values that men embrace, they will have a certain advantage in this endeavor.

For instance, aggressiveness, which has become distorted within the masculinity rite to mean violence and unprincipled egotism, might be developed by women as the energetic and optimistic pursuit of a goal.

Competition could be seen as a challenge that exacts the best efforts of each individual, rather than as an anxiety-ridden, winner-take-all contest.

Physical strength and skill could be viewed not as masculine prerogatives, not as badges of dominance or as weapons to achieve victory, not as peripheral attributes, but as integral to the personality and accomplishments of each individual—the mirror image of the psyche.

Those women who decide to develop these qualities, on their own terms, can make good use of the other so-called feminine traits to which they have been conditioned for so long—patience, supportiveness, a propensity for strategy and manipulation. For men will continue to manipulate women according to the old rules. And in their careers, at least, in order to survive and achieve, women may have to respond with manipulation of their own: a calculated appraisal of where men's heads are and how best to turn them. In this limited way—when there is no other way—some of the old tactics will inevitably be used.

"I have nothing but respect," Gloria Steinem has said, "for women who win the game with rules given them by the enemy."[4]

184

She was referring to Jacqueline Onassis, and many women would think the compliment misplaced. It seems likely, in fact, that in the not-so-distant future women who continue to play the game with each other and with men in order to vicariously advance their own status will elicit amusement and pity more often than respect. As the falseness of the old roles becomes more and more apparent, women who continue to hide behind them will seem superfluous, out of place—like costumed Halloween tricksters ringing a doorbell at high noon in midsummer. Except for their theatrical value, such postures will not be worthy of notice, for there will be little of the women behind them *to* notice. Indeed, one can already see this happening. Where dedicated game players were once objects of jealousy, they are now often ignored by other women or addressed with a measure of contempt.

Once women begin actively to seek power, to seize the offensive, they will be formidable opponents. As newcomers to the establishment, they are not jaded by corrupt precedent nor lulled into dreary acceptance of the status quo. They are anxious to take on City Hall, to challenge the worst aspects of male authority—the corruption, the deceit, the arrogance—and to assert their own authority. And with their new awareness of the hypocrisy of their own roles, women should become increasingly sensitive to the charades of others.

As they seek to gain power, women might best begin by concentrating on issues that unite rather than divide them—issues important to everyone (like inflation, financial security, the incredible cost of medical care, child care, the problems of the old, blue-collar boredoom, shorter work weeks and more varied work schedules, the environment). Bringing down the price of meat is an immediately relevant and nondivisive issue, and the woman-led meat boycott showed that women from all levels of society can act in unison.

On an individual level, women can start now to learn to win without guilt and lose without rancor—and to keep up the process until their goals are achieved. Sport, reflecting as it does the physical bias against women and the masculinity rite that perpetuates it, is an ideal area in which women can practice changing personal as well as national policies. One of the reasons men put women down professionally is that they have been conditioned to put them down physically.

On a group level, women need to get together often—not only in consciousness-raising sessions but in gyms and poolhalls, on recreation fields and tennis courts; places where they can admire each other's physical skills and improve their own. Learning to win, lose, and cooperate in play situations will make it easier for them to do the same elsewhere.

Where can they play? Women who live in a small town or in the suburbs might petition the council for permission to use the recreation halls and fields on a regular basis. They could start a girls' baseball team—or support, by writing to their congressmen, current efforts to have girls admitted to the Little League. A woman who really wants some fireworks might join, or try to join, her local fire department. (Or at least petition for the auxiliary's right to use the men's recreational facilities at the fire hall.)

City women could try tackling those athletic facilities, such as poolhalls, that by written or unwritten code are traditionally "for men only." (That would make the furor over New York's McSorley's Ale House seem faint in comparison.) A bit of advice, though: women who can't play well shouldn't be the ones to crash the gate. Instead, they should first send in an elite corps of players capable of beating the men as well as joining them.

And any woman, remembering how important sport is as a social conditioner, can develop an active interest in all phases of it. If she's watching a pro game, she can start appraising individual performances rather than taking sides. In her own games, she should not be so intent on winning that the good form of the opposition goes unappreciated (and unlearned from).

Competing with a man in one-to-one games can yield a number of psychological insights, as some marriage counselors have learned. And in view of the uncertain theoretical leanings of many psychiatrists, an hour at the pool table or on the tennis courts may prove more therapeutic than a session on the couch. Though this may seem to be a simple-minded solution to problems, games *are* a microcosm of life-styles; and women will find that they behave much the same way outside the confines of a game.

Some of the revelations can be painful. Fear of success, for instance. Because women aren't used to competing, they're often embarrassed winners as well as bad losers. It takes a special effort for most women to win, whether against a man or against a female friend, without feeling twinges of guilt—as it does to lose without feeling either relieved or angry. Sometimes a woman will discover that she literally can't win. After running all the balls but one at pool, she may find herself mysteriously unable to sink the eight. Until then, she's played well, but on that decisive shot she plays like a beginner. She should ask herself why. Perhaps she feels she can't be *that* good—or that winning will cost her social approval—or perhaps lead others to expect that she will win again, making failure more painful?

Is she taking the game and/or herself too seriously? Is

she demoralized by criticism, deflated by laughter over a missed shot, self-conscious about how she looks to others? Does she feel, after losing, like braining her male partner with a cue stick or a tennis racket? Well, maybe he's played for two years and she's played for two months; maybe he's had more access to the game than she has, a background of competitive sport that she missed. Unfair? Of course. But there's always another game, and she can *learn*. Once she does, she'll be able to relax and take pleasure in a game well played, no matter who comes out on top.

Psychological gamesmanship works both ways. When playing against some men, women find that their sex becomes an automatic psychological advantage. Most men who think women are inferior will, when outplayed by them, perform poorly. On the other hand, a woman may find herself getting rattled and playing badly if a man takes a condescending interest in her game—or, as sometimes happens, loses deliberately to her. A patronizing attitude can be hell on self-confidence, which is one reason so many women have so little of it.

A woman romantically interested in a man might try challenging him to a competitive game like wrestling—or, at least, arm wrestling. She'll know the man better after one night of games than after two or three dinner dates.

On a national level, realizing the value of competition as a model for achievement, women can work to improve their status in organized sport. Already, there are some hopeful signs:

Around the country, community recreation programs and country clubs are promoting coed games for adolescents and teenagers—softball, bowling, volleyball, and tennis. YMCA's and YWCA's have introduced coed and family programs. High schools are awarding major letters in sports to females.

In New York State, the laws prohibiting girls from competing on boys' teams in noncontact sports were abolished as a result of a year-long experiment at a hundred schools throughout the state. "Competing against boys was not harmful, physically, emotionally or socially," reported *Today's Health* in April 1971. The article added that only 5 per cent of the girls polled in the experiment considered mixed competition to be too strenuous.

In April 1973, eleven coeds from two southern Florida colleges (Broward County Community College and Marymount College) won the right to participate in intercollegiate events on tennis scholarships. The decision was the result of a federal court suit brought by the coeds against the National Educational Association and its affiliates, charged with discrimination in enforcing a prohibition against athletic scholarships for women.

At the Community College in Coos Bay, Oregon, Fran Sichting has become one of the few female athletes competing on a men's track team against men in intercollegiate competition.

In Connecticut an agreement was reached early in 1973 between the Connecticut Interscholastic Athletic Conference and the state Civil Liberties Union, allowing girls to compete with boys in a variety of noncontact sports where no team program exists for women. The agreement, in U.S. District Court, was the result of a suit by two Connecticut girls against the principals of the high schools they attend, the boards of education for these schools, and the CIAC. Under the new ruling, girls may compete with boys in track, golf, tennis, cross-country, gymnastics, and swimming.

Women's rowing, according to an item in *Time* magazine (May 7, 1973), is "scudding along at an astonishing pace." In New England there are all-girl crews at Radcliffe, Wellesley, Yale, MIT, and Wesleyan. The best of the lot compete at the Women's National Regatta, getting a chance at the European championships in Moscow and perhaps an eventual crack at the 1976 Olympics. There—thanks largely to the persistence of Ingrid Duseldorp, the European sculling champion—women's rowing crews will be a scheduled event for the first time.

The Association of Intercollegiate Athletics for Women, founded in 1972, is taking control of women's college sports out of the hands of men. The AIAW, which sponsors golf, swimming, badminton, gymnastics, track and field, basketball, and volleyball, wants to shift the emphasis from money and professionalism to the rewards to be found within the sport itself, to the satisfactions of individual accomplishment.

Oberlin College, the oldest coeducational college in the United States, is now working to make all of its programs equal in funds, coaching, and equipment, thanks to the athletic direction of Jack Scott. He and his wife, Micki, founded the Institute for the Study of Sport and Society to keep tabs on discriminatory national sports policies.

Yale University recently appointed a woman, Joni Barrett, as its athletic director.

In July 1973, University of Indiana football coach Lee Corso announced, "The next assistant coach I hire will be a woman."

In California, the Junior College Athletic Association voted in 1973 to allow mixed competition in noncontact sports.

Suzy Chaffee has organized the World Sports Foundation for the Modernization of Sport, and was also named to the board of directors of the U.S. Olympic Committee.

In September 1972, the Eastern College Conference on Athletics declared undergraduate women eligible for all varsity intercollegiate noncontact sports played by its 214 colleges and universities. (Each college, however, still has the right to decide whether to let women play.)

Elsewhere, dozens of court battles are being waged and protests staged to try to correct athletic inequalities.[5]

The fight to admit girls to the Little League continues. In Ypsilanti, Michigan, the City Council is taking the National Little League to federal court for its refusal to let twelve-year-old Carolyn King play for its local team, the Orioles. Carolyn, who beat out fifteen boys to qualify for a starting position in the outfield, has precedents on her side. Courts in Michigan and nine other Midwestern states have banned sex discrimination in athletics supported by state funds. In virtually every state, suits have been brought to end discrimination in high school athletic programs. And adult women athletes are starting to be heard in their demand for equal treatment: at the 1972 American Athletic Union-sponsored marathon in New York's Central Park, women runners sat out the "women only" race, and when the men got up to run, they ran too. At Forest Hills in 1973, men and women received equal prize money.

Women don't want to imitate men's sports any more than they want to imitate men. They do want an opportunity to compete on the same level, and to create in the process a new game that has no boundaries, no hard and fast rules, no automatic losers. Anyone can play.

A dentist in southern Michigan moved his practice to northern Michigan so his wife and daughter could benefit from year-round sports.

A sixteen-year-old girl was asked by her father, "What would you like for your birthday?" Her reply: "Pierced ears, two sets of earrings, a sweat suit, and a pair of track shoes." She got them.

A former Miss America whose winning talent was playing the piano is now also known in her community for her expertise in handling horses and teaching riding.

A woman who took up golf late in life was determined to play the game until she broke one hundred. In her seventieth year she did.

Important steps are being taken toward winning self-awareness, confidence, new interests, and, above all, joy in living.

Perhaps when women accomplish their goals, they can do something to change the nature of man's game—and the world.

APPENDIX I

The following recommendations were adopted at a NOW Sports and Athletics Workshop in March 1973:

1. Publicity, *full coverage,* and emphasis on *women's sports events* in newspapers, TV, radio, and other media must be improved and vastly expanded.

2. More *female officials* (umpires, referees) must be trained and employed in all sports areas—women's sports, men's sports, coed events.

3. *Personnel.* In addition to more female officials, there is a need for more female sportswriters, sportscasters, editors. More female athletic directors and supervisors are urgently needed (department chairmen, directors, bureaus of health and physical education), female personnel in after-school programs, afternoon and evening centers, and community education programs are badly needed.

4. *Facilities.* Facilities, equipment, expenses, priorities must be greatly improved and equalized in the area of women's sports. The often inferior or missing facilities for women's programs and events in relation to men's events can no longer continue.

5. *Funding.* Along with facilities and equipment, female events and programs need to be funded and maintained on the same level as men's programs and coed programs. Numbers of teams, sessions, personnel, publicity must be the same for men's and women's sports.

6. *Coaching.* Women's teams should be equal in emphasis, support, seriousness as men's teams. Opportunities for girls and women to join coed teams or women's teams with equity of numbers of teams available, types of sports covered by the team programs, and sessions available must be expanded. Pay for female coaches must be the same as for male coaches.

7. *Physical-education classes.* Program and curriculum should offer equal opportunities and emphasis for both female and male students. Coed classes would help greatly in this area (often boys receive little or no exposure to such activities as dance, while many girls' programs offer dance activities and emphasize little else).

8. *Health classes (hygiene).* Here, too, coed classes would be beneficial to all students, and to all teaching personnel in the field. Classes in sex education, family living, drug abuse, etc., can easily be coed.

9. *Female athletes* must have the same opportunities to excel in amateur and professional athletics events. Professional women athletes should be given the same opportunities to gain the same money opportunities (winning prize money, etc., business contacts) as the male athlete.

10. *Stereotyping.* Female sports participants and competitors must no longer be labeled or stereotyped as "masculine," tomboy, unladylike, or unfeminine when they participate and excel and enjoy sports and athletic events. Pride in athletic development, skill, and excellence must be

valued and encouraged in female athletes as well as in male athletes.

11. *Recreation*. Recreational skills and participation must be encouraged, and opportunities to participate must be available for all students, male and female. Recreational events usually are good coed activities.

APPENDIX II

The following works of art from classical antiquity portray physically active women. Until now they and many others have been overlooked by the vast majority of scholars.

ASHMOLEAN MUSEUM, *Oxford*

Sarcophagus	"The Hunt of the Calydonian Boar," late second century A.D., Cook Collection, Michaelis, no. 57
Statue	"Wounded Amazon," late fifth century B.C. Roman copy of Greek original, Michaelis, no. 24
Sarcophagus fragment	"Children at Play," first to second century A.D. Michaelis, no. 107

BRITISH MUSEUM, *London*

Votive Relief 790	Cyrene crowned by Libya
Sculpture 910	Nereid
Sculpture 1022	Frieze of mausoleum, "Greeks and Amazons"
Sculpture 1432	Cyrene (?)
Sculpture 1472	Cyrene
Sculpture 1384	Cyrene and lion

Terracottas

TC-1907-5-17-1	"Thetis on Seahorse"
C-41	"Boy and Girl Wrestling"
615	"Peleus and Thetis"

Bronzes

561	"Heracles and Auge. Female Archers"
560	"Amazons"
638	"Nereids"
640	"Nereids Riding Sea Monsters"
748	"Peleus and Atalanta Wrestling"
746	"Achilles and Penthesileia"
	"Peleus and Atalanta"
751	"Greeks and Amazons"
667	Candelabrum, "Peleus and Thetis"
285	Siris Bronze, Shoulder piece from a cuirass
1913	Mirror, "Penthesileia"
1966	Mirror, "Peleus and Thetis"

Vases	Hercules and Amazons—B 164, B 154, B 315, B 217, B 218, B 219, B 426, B 463, B 472, B 495, B 496, B 535, B 534, B 600, B 601, B 634, B 635, B 533, E 45, E 167
	Achilles and Penthesileia—B 209, B 210, B 322, B 323, E 280
	Peleus and Thetis—B 349, B 215, B 298, B 465, B 500, B 540, B 449, B 619, E 424, E 15, E 772 (Thetis), E 472
	Amazons, E 45
Gem	Portland Vase #4036, "Peleus and Thetis"

THE LOUVRE, *Paris*

958	Sarcophagus fragment, "Atalanta and Meleagre"
324	Stele, possibly "Zeus, Hera, and Thetis"

2437	Funerary stele, "Cyrene"
3563	Funerary stele, "Cyrene"
3489	Funerary stele, "Cyrene"
MA801	Funerary stele, "Cyrene"
2119	Sarcophagus, "Achilles and Penthesileia"
396	Sarcophagus, "Nereids"
1634	Sarcophagus, "Nereids"
440	Sarcophagus, "Nereids"
1052	Sarcophagus, "Achilles and Penthesileia"
404	Bas-relief, "Greeks and Amazons"
14	Bas-relief, "Greek and Amazon"
522	Statue, "Atalanta," third century B.C.
331	Statue, "Amazone Blessée," right breast exposed

Vases

G 53	"Peleus and Thetis"
G 373	"Peleus and Thetis"
G 65	"Peleus and Thetis"
S1677	"Greeks and Amazons"
F 203	"Amazons"
E 643	"Nereids and Achilles"

CAPITOLINE MUSEUM, *Rome*

1378	Sarcophagus, "Nereids," second century A.D.
917	Sarcophagus, "Atalanta and Boar Hunt," third century A.D.
1897	Sarcophagus, "Atalanta and Boar Hunt"
3	Relief, "Boar Hunt"
70	Sarcophagus, "Greeks and Amazons"
1	Statue, "Amazonne Ferita"
19	Statue, "Amazonne"
651	Statue, "Amazonne"
2269	Sarcophagus, "Nereids," second century A.D.

METROPOLITAN MUSEUM OF ART, *New York*

Bronze   Female Acrobats 46, 11.6 and 09.221.13

Vases   Hearst Collection, "Peleus and Thetis," Altamura painter

Hearst Collection, "Nereids on Dolphins," red-figured vase by Eretria painter

Hearst Collection, "Peleus and Thetis," red-figured vase by the Chicago painter

Hydria, Attic, 500 B.C., Berlin painter "Achilles and Penthesileia," 10.210.19

Stamnos, Attic, 470 B.C., "Peleus and Thetis," 56.171.51

Lekythoi, "Peleus, Thetis, Nereids," 41.162.207

Bronze mirror, Etruscan, 400–350 B.C., "Peleus Surprising Thetis at Her Bath," 19.221.16

THE VATICAN, *Rome*

4968	Relief, "Atalanta and Boar Hunt"
727	Statue, "Roman Woman with Mask and Club of Hercules"
3366	Sculpture, fragment of Sarcofago Chigi, man swording a woman
10567	Sarcophagus, "Nereids and Triton"
9879	Sculpture fragment, "Nereid Riding Sea Monster"
748	Statue, "Wounded Amazon"
69	Sarcophagus, "Greeks and Amazons"
61	Sarcophagus, "Nereids Riding Sea Monsters"
54	Sarcophagus fragment, "Greeks and Amazons"
49	Sarcophagus, "Greeks and Amazons"

200

37	Statue, "Amazon," right breast exposed
67	Statue, "Amazon," left breast exposed
2784-85	Statue, "Girl Runner"
13887	Alabaster box, men and women fighting
18216	Vase, man about to sword a woman
17954	Vase, man about to seize a woman

NOTES

Chapter 1. CINDERELLA WAS A WINNER

1. "Adam Smith," *The Money Game,* New York, Dell, p. 106.
2. The criteria used to define life games by Eric Berne in *Games People Play.*
3. Helene Deutsch, *The Psychology of Women,* Vol. 1, p. 251.
4. "Radcliffe's President Matina Horner," *New York Times Magazine,* January 14, 1973. Also "Femininity and Successful Achievement," a research study conducted at the University of Michigan, quoted in *Parade,* July 9, 1972.
5. Dr. John Kane. From authors' notes at Penn State Conference on Women and Sport, August 1972.
6. John M. Roberts and Brian Sutton-Smith, "Child Training and Game Involvement," *Sport, Culture and Society,* p. 126.
7. Brian Sutton-Smith with John M. Roberts and Robert Kozelka, "Game Involvement in Adults," *Sport, Culture and Society,* p. 253.
8. Roger Caillois, "The Structure and Classification of Games," *Sport, Culture and Society,* p. 49.
9. From authors' notes at Penn State Conference on Women and Sport, August 1972.
10. Sigmund Freud, *New Introductory Lectures in Psychoanalysis,* p. 184.

Chapter 2. GETTING SICK OF THE GAME

1. Margaret Mitchell, *Gone With the Wind,* p. 79.
2. Marion Harland, *Eve's Daughters,* p. 57.
3. Data on female mental hospital admissions from Phyllis Chesler's *Women and Madness,* p. 318.
4. According to a telephone interview with James Lowe, head of public relations for the National Council on Alcoholism.

5. Statistics drawn from report by presidential Council of Economic Advisors, reported in *Time*, February 12, 1973.

6. Simone de Beauvoir, *The Second Sex*, p. 330.

7. June Wilson, syndicated column appearing in *Des Moines Register*, March 17, 1962.

8. Arthritis may occur when individuals become suddenly inactive as adults after a childhood and youth of intense physical activity or if they suppress aggressive instincts. Dr. Boslooper has interviewed six women who contracted arthritis after the age of twenty. In all cases they had a negative physical orientation resulting, variously, from traumatic physical experiences or criticism of their activities and attitudes about competition and aggression and followed by relative inactivity as adults.

9. Chesler, op. cit., p. 49.

10. Abraham Maslow, "Self-esteem (Dominance Feeling) and Sexuality in Women," *Journal of Social Psychology*, 16, 1942, pp. 259ff.

11. Betty Friedan, "Up from the Kitchen Floor," *New York Times Magazine*, March 4, 1973.

12. Chesler, op. cit., p. 51.

13. Lucinda Franks, "See Jane Run," *Ms.*, January 1972.

Chapter 3. THE PHYSICAL BIAS

1. F. Scott Fitzgerald, *The Great Gatsby*, p. 17.

2. Ibid., p. 59.

3. Germaine Greer, *The Female Eunuch*, p. 56 (Bantam edition).

4. Susan Brownmiller, "Street Fighting Woman," *New York Times* op-ed page, April 18, 1973.

5. From a review of *The Secret Power of Femininity* (American Family and Femininity Institute, P.O. Box 794, San Gabriel, California) on the *New York Times* women's page, August 6, 1972.

6. Esther Vilar, *The Manipulated Man*, pp. 33–34.

7. Simone de Beauvoir, *The Second Sex*, p. 332.

8. Marie Hart, "Women Sit at the Back of the Bus," *Psychology Today*, October 1971.

9. Jack Scott, "Women in Sport," *Win*, April 1972.

10. Frank Deford, "What Makes Robyn Ride," article in *Sports Illustrated* condensed for *Reader's Digest*, December 1972.

11. Fred V. Hein, quoted in *Today's Health*, October 1967.

Chapter 4. THE FEMININE PHYSIQUE

1. Paul Weiss, *Sport: A Philosophic Inquiry*.

2. Ibid.

3. Clelia D. Mosher, M.D., "The Muscular Strength of College Women," *Journal of the American Medical Association,* Vol. 70, No. 3, January 19, 1918. According to Dr. John Kane, who reported at the Penn State Conference on Women and Sport that he had been unable to find any such studies in the literature.

4. From authors' notes, Penn State Conference on Women and Sport, August 1972.

5. From Dr. Boslooper's notes on Conference on Women and Girls in Sport and Play at the American Association for the Advancement of Science annual meeting, December 1968, in Dallas, Texas.

6. Daniel Druheim and Carl E. Klafs, "The Star Spangled Scramble," *Psychology Today,* September 1972.

7. From authors' notes at the Penn State Conference on Women and Sport, August 1972.

8. Dr. Julia Sherman, quoted in a press release from the University of Wisconsin at Madison, February 1973.

9. Robert Briffault, *The Mothers: The Matriarchal Theory of Social Origins.*

10. Gyula Erdelyi, M.D., "Gynecological Survey of Female Athletes," *Journal of Sports, Medicine and Physical Fitness,* Vol. 2, No. 3, September 1962, pp. 174–77.

11. Drs. Franz Alexander and Boris B. Rubenstein, quoted in *Family Health,* November 1971.

12. Dr. Ferguson Anderson, also quoted in above article.

13. Grace Fischer in speech to the American Heart Association convention, May 6, 1972.

14. Elizabeth Gould Davis mentions this theory in her book *The First Sex* ("Fetishes and Their Origins"). The unluckiness of the number has also been attributed to Judas's numerical rank. But if the number had not already borne a stigma it seems unlikely that anyone would have noticed he was the thirteenth disciple.

15. Study cited in "Sporting Activities During Pregnancy," *Journal of Obstetrics and Gynecology,* Vol. 32, No. 5, November 1968.

16. Weiss, op. cit.

Chapter 5. GAMES WOMEN CAN'T PLAY

1. In a telephone interview with Creighton Hale of the Little League's National Offices, August 1972.

2. Olga Connally, interview quoted in *New York Times,* July 15, 1972.

3. *Seventeen,* June 1971.

4. Jack Scott, "America's Masculinity Rite," *Win* magazine, May 1972.

5. Eileen Portz, "The Influence of Siblings, Sex, and Birth Order on Participation in Sports." From authors' notes at the Penn State Conference on Women and Sport, August 1972.

6. Carol Mann, to Associated Press reporter Cynthia Lowry.
7. Lucinda Franks, "See Jane Run," *Ms.*, January 1973.

Chapter 6. BLOOMER GIRLS, TOMBOYS, AND YANKEE DOODLE DANDIES

1. Dr. Boslooper's notes at the Second World Symposium on the History of Sport and Physical Education at Banff, Alberta, Canada, June 1971. Harold A. Harris, "Amateur and Professional in Greek and Roman Sport."
2. Elizabeth Halsey, *Women in Physical Education*, pp. 124ff.
3. Ibid.
4. Sarah Berenson, "Basketball for Women," *Physical Education*, 3 (September 1894), p. 106.
5. From personal conversations between historian Douglas Miller of Michigan State University and Marcia Hayes. See also J.C. Furnas, *The Americans: A Social History of the United States, 1587–1914*, p. 102.
6. Quoted by Ann Hall at the Second World Symposium on the History of Sport and Physical Education. "The Role of the Safety Bicycle in the Emancipation of Women."
7. Ibid.
8. Ibid.
9. *Windsong: An Aviation Salute*, prepared for the International Explorers' Club annual convention, December 10, 1968.
10. C. W. Hackensmith, *The History of Physical Education*, p. 411.
11. *New York Times*, October 23, 1922.
12. Hackensmith, ibid.
13. Fortunately a woman had the last word. Almost a half century later, in June 1972, Celler faced Elizabeth Holtzman in the New York City Democratic primary. He compared her campaign efforts to that of a "toothpick trying to topple the Washington Monument." The monument subsequently toppled.

Chapter 7. THE MASCULINITY RITE

1. University of Michigan Research Center, public-relations release about a survey of public attitudes to the Vietnam War, July 1972.
2. *New York Times*, January 13, 1973.
3. Alex Natan, "Sport and Politics," in *Sport, Culture and Society*, p. 206.
4. Column in *Glamour* magazine, October 1972.
5. Douglas Looney, "Sunday's Warriors," *The National Observer*, December 2, 1972.
6. Jack Scott, "America's Masculinity Rite," *Win*, May 1972.

7. Morton Golden, quoted in *Glamour,* October 1972.

8. Helen Lippincott, "Male Chauvinism at Candlestick Park," *San Francisco Bay Guardian,* December 22, 1971.

9. To our knowledge there is only one female sports columnist, Caroline Kane, who writes for the *Long Island Press.*

10. Quoted from Lee Arthur's report to the NOW Task Force on Sports, February 1973.

11. Ernest Remits, *The Feeling of Superiority and Anxiety-Superior,* the Ottawa Trial Survey on Personality, pp. 1, 21.

12. Bruce C. Ogilvie and Thomas Tutko, "If You Want to Build Character, Try Something Else," *Psychology Today,* October 1971.

Chapter 8. HOW THE GAME BEGAN

1. Book I, translated by Arthur S. Way, The Loeb Classical Library, p. 39.

2. "Physiognomics," Vol. 2, in *Minor Works,* translated by W.S. Hett, Loeb Classical Library, pp. 95, 111.

3. Most notably Procopius of Caesarea (527–565 A.D.), who insisted that the Amazons never existed. "Procopius," Vol. 5, *History of the Wars,* translated by H. B. Dewing, p. 77.

4. Elizabeth Gould Davis, *The First Sex.*

5. The Amazonian tradition is integral to the history of the Greeks and to the philosophy of Western civilization. Greek history is recorded in four great epic conflicts: battles between the Gods and the Giants, between the Greeks and the Persians, between Attalides and the Gauls, and between the Greeks and the Amazons. The Greeks always emerge as winners of these legendary conflicts, as if they were trying to convince themselves of their indominability and the right to exist without a threat to their power.

6. "The Geography of Strabo," Vol. 4, translated by Horace Leonard Jones, The Loeb Classical Library, 11.V.2, p. 233.

7. Dietrich Von Bothmer, "Amazons in Greek Art," *Bulletin,* Metropolitan Museum of Art, March 1957.

8. In 440 B.C., four principal sculptured pieces of Amazon women were made in competition between the artists Polykleitos, Pheidias, Kresilas, and Phradmon. The works were to be displayed in the temple of Artemis at Ephesus, and it was required that the sculptors include the essential features of the traditional concept of the Amazons. (Adolf Furtwängler, *Masterpieces of Greek Sculpture.*) All the resulting sculptures are full-bosomed.

9. The three groups of Amazons Diodorus wrote about were the Libyan Amazons, those who were "about the Thermadon River," and "those

who disappeared entirely many generations before the Trojan War." "Diodorus of Sicily," Vol. 2, the Loeb Classical Library, Book 3, p. 247. (In the sixteenth century Francesco de Orellana saw warlike women who reminded him of the women of the ancient stories while exploring the mouth of a river in South America; hence, the river, the Amazon, now bears their name.)

10. J. J. Bachofen, *Myth, Religion and Mother Right*, translated by Ralph Manheim, p. 71.

11. *Plutarch's Lives*, E. T. by Bernadotte Perrin, The Loeb Classical Library, Vol. 1, XXVI, p. 59.

12. *Apollodorus: The Library*, XXV.9, translated by James G. Frazer, The Loeb Classical Library, p. 203.

13. The most remarkable episode recorded by Diodorus (Book 2, p. 31) concerns the encounter of the Amazons with the Persians: "Cyrus, the King of the Persians, the mightiest ruler of his day, made a campaign with a vast army into Scythia. The queen of the Scythians not only cut the army of the Persians to pieces, but she even took Cyrus prisoner and crucified him; and the nation of the Amazons, after it was organized, was so distinguished for its manly prowess that it not only overran much of the neighboring territory but even subdued a large part of Europe and Asia." The historicity of this episode is almost impossible to determine. But even as fiction, it demonstrates the remarkable influence these women had on the Greeks.

14. Book I, p. 55.

15. The root of the word Atalanta means "equal" or "equal in weight" or "endurance." The myth is another version of the Amazon theme. In the Penthesileia story the woman is deceived by the man, who has deceived himself. In the Atalanta story both Atalanta and Melanion are deceived by love and sex.

16. See *The Scythians* by Tamara Talbot Rice.

17. P. 41.

18. Associated Press story in the *San Francisco Chronicle,* March 28, 1972, p. 21.

19. Edward Carpenter, *Love's Coming of Age.*

20. P. 95.

21. P. 75.

22. Euripides, *Andromache,* quoted in Charles Seltman's *Women in Antiquity.*

23. P. 75.

24. "Memorabilia and Oeconomicus," translated by E. C. Marchant, The Loeb Classical Library, p. 421.

25. "Physiognomics," Vol. 2, in *Minor Works,* translated by W. S. Hett, The Loeb Classical Library, p. 95, 111. "Generation of Animals" IV.vi, translated by A.S. Peck, The Loeb Classical Library, p. 459.

26. "The Republic," Book 5, Modern Student's Library, pp. 192ff.

27. The same issue—property—was behind many of the Salem witch trials. Many so-called witches were women of property; accusations of satanic possession proved a convenient way to get possessions from them. (From conversations between Marcia Hayes and author Walter Gibson, an authority on witchcraft.)

28. William Sprague, *The Excellent Woman.*

29. *Paracelsus,* Jolande Jacobi, editor, Bollingen Series, Vol. 28.

Chapter 9. THE PSYCHOLOGICAL BIAS

1. Sigmund Freud, "Some Psychological Consequences of the Anatomical Distinction Between the Sexes," *Collected Papers,* Vol. 5, pp. 191, 197.

2. Joseph Rheingold, *The Fear of Being a Woman,* p. 714.

3. Bruno Bettelheim, "The Commitment Required of a Woman Entering a Scientific Profession in Present Day Society," *Women and the Scientific Professions,* from an M.I.T. symposium on American Women in Science and Engineering.

4. Eric Erikson, "Inner and Outer Space: Reflections on Womanhood," *Daedalus,* Vol. 3, 1965.

5. Columbia University course audited by Marcia Hayes in 1968–69.

6. Phyllis Chesler, *Women and Madness,* p. 54.

7. This tendency of psychologists to examine only those myths and legends that portray a male-oriented viewpoint is exemplified in Robert Donnington's book *Wagner's "Ring" and Its Symbols,* a psychological analysis of the Niebelungenlied in terms of Jung's archetypal constructs. Because Donnington's book was based on the Scandinavian version rather than the German version of the legend, it was definitely not helpful to women.

8. P. 46.

9. Other contributions have been made by Viola Klein in *The Feminine Character;* John Weir Perry in *Psychotherapy of the Psychoses;* Natalie Shainess in "Newer Concepts of Feminine Personality," *Diseases of the Nervous System,* Vol. 22, No. 1, January 1961; Ignacio Matte-Blanco, M.D., in "The Constitutional Approach to the Study of Human Personality," *Psychiatric Research Reports,* December 1955; and Arthur Burton and Robert Kantor in "The Touching of the Body," *The Psychoanalytic Review,* spring 1964.

Chapter 10. ACHILLES INCARNATE

1. "Sadism, Masochism, and Aggression," Vol. 31.

2. Vincent Canby, *New York Times,* July 30, 1972.

3. Victoria Sullivan, *New York Times,* August 27, 1972.

4. Phyllis Chesler, *Women and Madness,* p. 155.

5. Helene Deutsch, *The Psychology of Women,* Vol. 1, p. 250.

6. Ibid., pp. 249–50.

7. Sullivan, op. cit.

8. Susan Brownmiller, "Street Fighting Woman," *New York Times* op-ed page, April 18, 1973.

9. Sophocles, "Electra," *The Complete Greek Drama,* Vol. 1, p. 539.

Chapter 11. THE NAKED APE ARGUMENT

1. Robert Ardrey, *African Genesis,* p. 165.

2. Desmond Morris, *The Naked Ape: A Zoologist's Study of the Human Animal,* p. 65.

3. Elaine Morgan, *The Descent of Woman,* pp. 17–22.

4. Lionel Tiger, *Men in Groups.*

5. The Tchambulian people live in New Guinea.

6. David Pilbeam, *New York Times Magazine,* September 3, 1972.

7. Just for the record, Beauvoir erred in her egg count. An African termite queen can, in fact, lay up to 7000 eggs a day—and lives as long as fifty years. (Courtesy of Rob Gannon, *What's Under a Rock?*)

8. E. W. Caspari, "The Evolutionary Importance of Sexual Processes of Sexual Behavior," *Sex and Behavior,* Frank Beach, editor, p. 40.

9. Dr. Edgar Berman, quoted in the *New York Times,* July 26, 1971.

10. J. L. Hampson, "Determinants of Psychosexual Orientation," *Sex and Behavior,* pp. 113–14.

11. Ibid., p. 121.

12. Margaret Mead, *Male and Female,* p. 277.

13. Hampson, ibid., p. 125.

Chapter 12. ENDGAME

1. Anselma del Olio, from an unpublished manuscript quoted by Phyllis Chesler in *Women and Madness,* pp. 270–71.

2. George Bernard Shaw.

3. Chesler, op. cit., pp. 292, 297.

4. Gloria Steinem, in *Time,* March 26, 1973.

5. For more guidelines on how to organize sports groups, information on what's being done and what should be done, write to: The Institute for the Study of Sport and Society, Hales Gymnasium, Oberlin, Ohio 44074, attention Micki Scott; or to Women's Athletic Association of San Jose, P.O. Box 24368, San Jose, California; or to the Task Force on Sports, NOW, 47 East 19th Street, New York, New York, attention Judy Wenning.

BIBLIOGRAPHY

Alland, Alexander, Jr., *The Human Imperative*, New York, Columbia University Press, 1972.

Ansbacher, Heinz and Rowena, *The Individual Psychology of Alfred Adler*, New York, Basic Books, 1956.

Ardrey, Robert, *African Genesis*, New York, Atheneum, 1961.

Bachofen, J. J., *Myth, Religion, and Mother Right*, Princeton, New Jersey, Princeton University Press, 1971.

Beach, Frank A., editor, *Sex and Behavior*, New York, John Wiley & Sons, Inc., 1965.

Beard, Mary R., *On Understanding Women*, Westport, Connecticut, Greenwood Press, Inc., 1931, 1968.

Berne, Eric, *Games People Play*, New York, Grove Press, 1964.

Bieber, Irving, et al., *Homosexuality: A Psychoanalytic Study of Male Homosexuals*, New York, Vintage Books, 1962.

Borgese, Elizabeth Mann, *Ascent of Woman*, New York, George Braziller, 1963.

Bragdon, Elizabeth, editor, *Women Today*, New York, The Bobbs-Merrill Company, 1953.

Briffault, Robert, *The Mothers*, New York, Macmillan Co., 1931.

Camden, Carroll, *The Elizabethan Woman*, New York and London, The Elsevier Press, 1952.

Carpenter, Edward, *Love's Coming of Age*, New York, Modern Library, 1911.

Carroll, Lewis, *Alice in Wonderland* (paperback edition), New York, E. P. Dutton.

Chase, George H., *Greek and Roman Sculpture in American Collections*, Harvard University Press, 1924.

Chesler, Phyllis, *Women and Madness*, Garden City, New York, Doubleday & Company, Inc., 1972.

Cunnington, C. Willett, *Women*, New York, Horizon Press, 1953.

Cureton, Thomas, *Physical Fitness and Dynamic Health*, New York, The Dial Press, 1965.

Davis, Elizabeth Gould, *The First Sex*, New York, G. P. Putnam's Sons, 1971.

De Beauvoir, Simone, *The Second Sex*, New York, Alfred A. Knopf, Inc., 1953.

Decter, Midge, *The New Chastity*, New York, Coward, McCann, and Geoghegan, Inc., 1972.

Deutsch, Helene, *The Psychology of Women*, New York, Grune & Stratton, Inc., 1945.

De Leeuw, Hendrik, *Woman: The Dominant Sex*, London, Yoseloff, 1957.

Dewing, H. B., *Procopius of Caesarea*, New York, G. P. Putnam's Sons, The Loeb Classical Library, 1928.

Diner, Helen, *Mothers and Amazons: The First Feminine History of Culture*, New York, Julian Press, 1969.

Dohen, Dorothy, *Women in Wonderland*, New York, Sheed and Ward, 1960.

Donaldson, James, *Woman*, London, Longmans, Green & Co., 1907.

Donington, Robert, *Wagner's "Ring" and Its Symbols*, New York, St. Martin's Press, 1963.

Dunbar, Janet, *The Early Victorian Woman*, London, George C. Harrap & Co., Ltd., 1953.

Edmonds, J. M., *The Greek Bucolic Poets*, New York, G. P. Putnam's Sons, The Loeb Classical Library, 1919.

———, *Lyra Graeca*, Vol. 3, New York, G. P. Putnam's Sons, The Loeb Classical Library, 1927.

Eliot, Charles, editor, *The Harvard Classics*, New York, P. F. Collier & Son Co., 1909.

Farnell, Lewis, *The Cults of the Greek States*, Oxford, the Clarendon Press, 1896.

Firestone, Shulamith, *The Dialectic of Sex: The Case for Feminist Revolution* New York, William Morrow and Company, 1970.

Fisher, Seymour, *The Female Orgasm,* New York, Basic Books, 1973.

Fitzgerald, F. Scott, *The Great Gatsby,* New York, Charles Scribner's Sons, 1925.

Flexner, Eleanor, *Century of Struggle,* Harvard University Press, 1959.

Frazer, James G., *Apollodorus: The Library,* Vol. 1, New York, G. P. Putnam's Sons, The Loeb Classical Library, 1921.

———, *Pausanias's Description of Greece,* Vol. 1, New York, G. P. Putnam's Sons, The Loeb Classical Library, 1898.

Freud, Sigmund, *New Introductory Lectures in Psychoanalysis,* New York, W. W. Norton, 1933.

Friedan, Betty, *The Feminine Mystique,* New York, W. W. Norton, 1963.

Furnas, J. C., *The Americans: A Social History of the United States, 1587–1914,* New York, G. P. Putnam's Sons, 1969.

Furtwängler, Adolf, *Masterpieces of Greek Sculpture,* New York, Charles Scribner's Sons, 1895.

Goldberg, Lucianne, and Sakol, Jeannie, *Purr, Baby, Purr: You Can Be Feminine, Liberated, Equal,* New York, Hawthorn Books, Inc., 1971.

The Golden Bough: A Study of Magic and Religion, Part 1, Vol. 2, London, Macmillan & Company, Ltd., 1911.

Graves, Robert, *The Greek Myths,* Part 2, London, Penguin Books, 1955.

———, *The White Goddess: a Historical Grammar of Poetic Myth,* New York, Farrar, Straus and Giroux, Inc., 1966.

Greer, Germaine, *The Female Eunuch,* New York, McGraw-Hill, 1971.

Gregory, Horace, *Metamorphoses* (Ovid), New York, Viking Press, 1958.

Gulick, Charles B., *Athenaeus,* Vol. 2, New York, G. P. Putnam's Sons, The Loeb Classical Library, 1928.

Hackensmith, C. W., *The History of Physical Education,* New York, Harper and Row, 1966.

Hackl, R., and N. Heaton, *Tiryns,* Athen, Eleutherondakis und Barth, Zweiter Band, 1912.

Halsey, Elizabeth, *Women in Physical Education,* New York, G. P. Putnam's Sons, 1961.

Harding, Mary Esther, *The Way of All Women*, New York, G. P. Putnam's Sons, for C. G. Jung Foundation for Analytical Psychology, 1970.

Harland, Marion, *Eve's Daughters*, New York, J. R. Anderson and H. S. Allen, 1882.

Harmon, A. M., *Lucian*, Vol. II, New York, G. P. Putnam's Sons, The Loeb Classical Library, 1919.

Havinghurst, Robert, et al., *The Potentialities of Women in the Middle Years*, East Lansing, Michigan, Michigan State University Press, 1956.

Hett, W. S., *Aristotle: Minor Works*, Vol. 1, Harvard University Press, The Loeb Classical Library, 1936.

Irwin, Inez Haynes, *Angels and Amazons*, New York, Doubleday & Company, Inc., 1933.

Jacobi, Jolande, editor, *Paracelsus*, Bollingen Series XXVIII, translated by Norbert Guterman, New York, Pantheon Books, 1958.

Jones, Horace L., *The Geography of Strabo*, Vol. 4, New York, G. P. Putnam's Sons, The Loeb Classical Library, 1927.

Jones, W. H. S., *Pausanias' Description of Greece*, Vol. 1, New York, G. P. Putnam's Sons, The Loeb Classical Library, 1918.

Jung, Carl G., *Contribution to Analytical Psychology*, New York, Harcourt, Brace, 1928.

————, *Man and His Symbols*, Garden City, New York, Doubleday & Company, Inc., 1964, 1969.

————, *Psyche and Symbol*, Garden City, New York, Doubleday & Company, Inc., 1958.

Kamiat, Arnold H., *Feminine Superiority and Other Myths*, New York, Bookman Associates, 1960.

Klein, Viola, editor, *The Feminine Character*, London, Kegan Paul, Trench, Trubner and Company, 1946.

Larousse Encyclopedia of Mythology (introduction by Robert Graves), New York, Prometheus Press, 1959.

Lettsom, William Nanson, *Niebelungenlied*, London, The Colonial Press, 1901.

Loy, John W., and Kenyon, Gerald S., editors, *Sport, Culture and Society*, New York, the Macmillan Company, 1969.

Lutz, Alma, *Created Equal*, Ann Arbor, Michigan, Finch Press Reprints, 1940.

216

McGovern, William Montgomery, *The Early Empires of Central Asia*, University of North Carolina Press, 1939.

Marchant, E. C., Xenophon's *Memorabilia and Oeconomicus*, New York, G. P. Putnam's Sons, The Loeb Classical Library, 1923.

May, Charles P., *Women in Aeronautics*, New York, Thomas Nelson and Sons, 1962.

Mead, Margaret, *Male and Female*, New York, William Morrow and Company, 1949.

Meggyesy, Dave, *Out of Their League*, New York, Paperback Library, 1972.

Meyer, Agnes E., *Out of These Roots*, Boston, Little, Brown and Company, 1953.

Miqueli, Violetta, *Women in Myth and History*, New York, Vantage Press, 1962.

Mitchell, Margaret, *Gone with the Wind*, New York, Macmillan Company, 1945.

Money, John, *Man and Woman, Boy and Girl: Differentiation and Dimorphism of Gender Identity*, Baltimore, Maryland, Johns Hopkins University Press, 1972.

Montagu, Ashley, *The Natural Superiority of Women*, New York, Macmillan Company, 1956.

Morgan, Elaine, *The Descent of Woman*, New York, Stein and Day, 1972.

Mull, Evelyn, *Women in Sports Car Competition*, New York, Arco, 1959.

Neumann, Erich, *Amor and Psyche*, London, Routledge and Kegan Paul, 1956.

Norlin, George, *Isocrates*, New York, G. P. Putnam's Sons, The Loeb Classical Library, 1918.

Noyes, Arthur P., M.D., *Noyes' Modern Clinical Psychiatry*, Laurence C. Kolb, editor, Philadelphia, W. B. Saunders and Company, 7th edition, 1968.

Oates, Whitney J., Eugene O'Neill, Jr., *The Complete Greek Drama*, Vol. 1, New York, Random House, 1938.

Oldfather, C. H., *Diodorus of Sicily*, Vol. 2, Harvard University Press, 1935.

Parker, Dr. Elizabeth, *The Seven Ages of Woman*, Baltimore, Maryland, The Johns Hopkins Press, 1960.

Parrish, Bernie, *They Call It a Game*, New York, The Dial Press, 1971.

Peck, A. C., *Generation of Animals* (Aristotle), Harvard University Press, 1943.

Perrin, Bernadotte, *Plutarch's Lives*, New York, Macmillan Company, Vol. I, XXVI, The Loeb Classical Library, 1914.

Perry, John Weir, *Psychotherapy of the Psychoses*, Arthur Burton, editor, New York, Basic Books, 1961.

Pfeiffer, John, *The Human Brain*, New York, Harper and Brothers, 1955.

Plato, *Republic*, introduction by Charles M. Bakewell, The Modern Student's Library, New York, Charles Scribner's Sons, 1928.

Proceedings of the First and Second World Symposiums on the History of Sport and Physical Education, 1968, 1971, Wingate Institute, Israel, and Banff, Alberta, Canada.

Rawlinson, George, *The History of Herodotus*, Vol. 1, New York, E. P. Dutton and Company, 1910.

Reich, Wilhelm, *The Function of the Orgasm*, New York, Farrar, Straus and Giroux, 1942.

Reik, Theodor, *The Search Within*, New York, Farrar, Strauss and Cudahy, 1956.

Remits, Ernest, *The Feeling of Superiority and Anxiety-Superior*, from the Ottawa Trial Survey on Personality, Ottawa, Runge Press, 1957.

Rheingold, Joseph, *The Fear of Being a Woman*, New York, Grune and Stratton, 1964.

Rice, Tamara Talbot, *The Scythians*, New York, Frederick A. Praeger, 1957.

Richter, Gisela, *A Handbook of Greek Art*, London, Phaidon Press, 1959.

———, *Red-figured Athenian Vases in the Metropolitan Museum of Art*, New Haven, Connecticut, Yale University Press, 1936.

———, *The Classical Periods in Greek Sculpture*, Oxford, The Clarendon Press, 1951.

Rodenwaldt, Gerhart, *Das Relief bei den Griechen*, Berlin, Schoetz und Parrhysius, 1923.

Roe, Dorothy, *The Trouble with Women Is Men*, Englewood Cliffs, New Jersey, Prentice-Hall, Inc., 1961.

Rogers, Agnes, *Women Are Here to Stay,* New York, Harper and Brothers, 1949.

Rostovtzeff, M., *Iranians and Greeks in Southern Russia,* Oxford, The Clarendon Press, 1922.

Sandys, Sir John, *The Odes of Pindar,* New York, G. P. Putnam's Sons, 1919.

Scott-Maxwell, Florida, *Women and Sometimes Men* (paperback) New York, Harper and Row, 1957, 1971.

Schwendener, Norma, *The History of Physical Education in the United States,* New York, A. S. Barnes and Company, 1942.

Seaton, R. C., *Apollonius Rhodius,* New York, Macmillan Company, The Loeb Classical Library, 1912.

Seltman, Charles, *Women in Antiquity,* New York, Collier Books, 1962.

Sherfy, Mary Jane, *The Nature and Evolution of Female Sexuality in Relation to Psychoanalytic Theory,* New York, Random House, 1972.

Shumway, Daniel, *The Niebelungenlied,* Boston, Houghton Mifflin Co., 1909.

Simeons, A. T. W., *Man's Presumptuous Brain: An Evolutionary Interpretation of Psychosomatic Disease* (paperback), New York, E. P. Dutton and Company, 1961.

"Smith, Adam" *The Money Game,* New York, Random House, 1969.

Sprague, William, *The Excellent Woman,* Boston, Gould and Lincoln, 1852.

Stebbins, Eunice Burr, *The Dolphin in the Literature and Art of Greece and Rome,* Menasha, Wisconsin, George Banta Publishing Company, 1929.

Stekel, Wilhelm, *Sadism and Masochism,* Vol. 1, New York, Liveright Publishing Company, 1929.

Tiger, Lionel, *Men in Groups,* New York, Random House, 1969.

Victory: How Women Won It, Woman Suffrage Association, Ann Arbor, Michigan, Finch Press Reprints, 1940.

Vilar, Esther, *The Manipulated Man,* New York, Farrar, Straus and Giroux, Inc., 1972.

Von Bothmer, Dietrich, *Amazons in Greek Art,* Oxford, The Clarendon Press, 1957.

Walker, Nicolette Milnes, *When I Put Out to Sea,* New York, Stein and Day, 1972.

Watts, A. E., *Metamorphoses,* Ovid, University of California Press, 1954.

Way, Arthur S., *The Fall of Troy,* Quintus Smyrnaeus, New York, Macmillan Company, The Loeb Classical Library, 1913.

Weiss, Paul, *Sport: A Philosophic Inquiry,* Urbana, Illinois, Southern Illinois University Press, 1969.

White, Hugh G. Evelyn, *The Homeric Hymns and Homerica,* Hesiod, New York, Macmillan Company, The Loeb Classical Library, 1914.

Williams, Roger J., *Biochemical Individuality,* New York, John Wiley and Sons, Inc., 1956.

Wright, Thomas, *Womankind in Western Europe,* London, Groombridge and Sons, 1869.

220

INDEX

Achilles, 120-21, 122, 146-47, 150
Adams, Bud, 108
Adombies, 63
Africa, 63, 104
African Genesis, 164
Afghanistan, 63
Age, 85-86
Aggressiveness and aggression, 31ff.,
    45, 59, 154, 167, 184. *See also* Com-
    petition; Sadism, Violence
Alabama, University of, 81-82
Albright, Tenley, 90
Alcoholism, 27, 29
Alexander, Franz, 64-65
Alexander the Great, 131-32
Alice's Adventures in Wonderland, 175
Alland, Alexander, 167
Allison, Roberta, 81-82
Amateur Athletic Union, 96, 98
Amazons, 116-26; Amazon complex, 146
American Cancer Society, 29
American Psychiatric Association, 143
Anderson, Clinton P., 109
Anderson, Ferguson, 65
Anderson, Gretta, 68
Androgen, 59, 60, 169
Andromache, 129-30
Anne, Princess, 77
Annie Get Your Gun, 22
Anthropology, 161, 162-74
Apes. *See* Primates
Arabs, 63
Ardrey, Robert, 163-64

Aristotle (Aristotelians), 56, 91, 115, 130,
    131, 133
Art works (sculpture, etc.), 116, 119, 197-
    201
Arteries, 65
Arthur, Lee, 108
Ashdown, Juliette, 108
Ashe, Arthur, 111
Ashira, the, 63
Ashmolean Museum, 197
Association of Intercollegiate Athletics
    for Women, 190
Atalanta, 121-22,129
Athens and Athenians, 118, 127ff. *See
    also* specific philosophers
Athletes. *See* Sport
Augustine, St., 134
Automobile driving. *See* Drivers and
    driving
Avengers, The, 79
Aviation. *See* Flying

Bachofen, J. J., 119-20
Baghdad, 73
Barrett, Joni, 190
Baseball, 57, 71-72, 78, 107, 110, 191. *See
    also* Little League
Baseball Writers' Association, 109
Basketball, 81, 83, 92, 98-99
Basketball for Women, 92
Baugh, Laura, 57-58
Beauvoir, Simone de, 31-32, 45, 77, 129,
    168

Berenson, Sarah, 92
Berk, Howard, 106
Berman, Edgar, 170
Berne, Eric, 139
Bethlehem, Penna., 81
Bettelheim, Bruno, 140
Bible (Old Testament), 132, 133
Bicycles, 93-94
Blackford, Mrs. Galen, 89-90
Blake, Ray, 81
Bloomer, Amelia, 93
Boats and sailing, 112, 113. *See also* Rowing
Bones, 58, 59
Books, 79
Borneo, 63
Boston Globe, 72
Boston Harbor, 68
Bothmer, Dietrich von, 118
Bragina, Ludmila, 87
Breasts, 164 ff.
Brick, Kay, 141
Bridges, Harry, 112
Bridges, Shirley, 112
Briffault, Robert, 63
British Museum, 116, 124, 197-98
Broward County Community College, 189
Brownmiller, Susan, 43, 157
Bruno, Giordano, 132
Bullfighting, 127
Bush, Jim, 84
Bushmen, 63

Caillois, Roger, 23
California, 93, 190
California, University of, at Los Angeles, 82-83
California Community College Association, 81
Calisthenics, 96-97
Camino, Paco, 127
Camp Fire Girls, 98
Canby, Vincent, 151
Cancer, 29
Capitoline Museum, 199
Captain Marvel, 79
Carpenter, Edward, 128
Carroll, Lewis, 175
Carson, Johnny, 32
Caspari, E. W., 169
Caulfield, John, 104

CBS, 108
Celler, Emanuel, 99
Chaffee, Suzy, 48, 53, 190
Champions, The, 79
Chastain, Jane, 108
Cheng, Chi, 47, 88
Chesler, Phyllis, 34, 36-37, 137, 141-42, 147, 153, 183
Christensen, Art, 81
Christianity (the Church), 132, 133-34
Chromosomes, 60-61, 138-39, 168
Cinderella, 22
Clockwork Orange, A (movie), 152
Coaching, 84, 106-7. *See also* specific coaches, sports
Cochrane, Jacqueline, 95-96
Colleges, 81-84, 91-92, 189-90 *See also* specific colleges, sports
Columbia University, 141
Compeorata de Athletismo de Europa, 66
Competition, 31-32, 110-12, 153ff., 184. *See also* Sports; specific sports
Cone, Caren, 82
Congo, the, 63
Connally, Olga, 74
Connecticut, 189
Cook, Sylvia, 113
Copernicus, 132
Coos Bay, Ore., 189
Cordero, Angel, 48
Corso, Lee, 190
Court, Margaret Smith, 75
Crete, 127
Crime, 110, 170
Curtiss, Glenn, 95
Cyrene, 123-24

Dallas Cowboys, 109
Darien, Conn., 57-58
Davis, Elizabeth Gould, 65, 117
Dawson, Buck, 47, 86
Dayaks, 63
Dearie, Gail, 48-49, 51
Debourse, Marie, 46
Decter, Midge, 177
Del Olio, Anselma, 179
Demaris, Ovid, 110
Dempsey, Jack, 67
Densmore, Dana, 178
Descent of Woman, The (Morgan), 164, 165-66

Deutsch, Helene, 18, 153ff.
De Varona, Donna, 47, 82
Diodorus, 119, 120, 124, 125
Division of labor, 63-64, 167-68
Donnelly, Marge, 41-42
Dorians, 117-18
Drew, Nancy (character), 79
Drivers and driving, 77, 94-95, 104
Druheim, Daniel, 61
Druses, 63
Duenkel, Ginny, 85
Duke University, 82
Duseldorp, Ingrid, 190

Eastern College Conference on Athletics, 190-91
Edmondson, J. Howard, 109
Egypt, ancient, 126-27
Endurance, 55, 58, 64ff., 85
Equal Rights Amendment, 99
Erdelyi, Gyula J., 64ff.
Erikson, Erik, 140, 147
Esquire, 110, 161
Estrogen, 59, 60, 64, 160, 171, 172
Euripides, 90-91, 129-30, 131
Evert, Chris, 47
Eve's Daughters, 27
Exercise (physical activity), 37-39, 41ff.
    (*See also* Sports); calisthenics, 97-99

Fairfax, John, 113
Fall of Troy, The, 115, 121
Fat, 62, 65
Fatigue, 36-37. *See also* Endurance
Female Eunuch, The, 42
Firestone, Shulamith, 138
First Sex, The. See Davis, Elizabeth Gould
Fischer, Grace, 65
Flying (aviation), 95-96, 141
Foltz, Vicki, 46-47
Football, 48-49, 102-3, 106ff.
Ford, Henry, 94
Franks, Lucinda, 39, 84
Frenzy (movie), 151-52, 155
Freud, Sigmund, and Freudians, 24-25, 56, 137ff., 146ff., 150
Friedan, Betty, 19, 35
Fromm, Erich, 147

Games, 18 ff., 31. *See also* Sports
Gargarians, 119
Genetics. *See* Chromosomes

Germans, 96
Gera, Bernice, 107
Gero, George, 150
Ghana, 104
Gibson Girls, 94
Girding up of loins, 133
Glamour, 41-42, 105-6
Goldberg, Lucianne, 32, 177-78
Golden, Morton, 107
Golf, 47, 57-58, 72-74, 84, 89-90
Gone with the Wind, 27
Good Housekeeping, 156
Great Gatsby, The, 41
Greeks, 90-91, 116ff.
Green Bay Packers, 106
Greer, Germaine, 42, 149
Gregario, Renee, 81
Griffin, Sunny, 159
Grossfeld, Muriel David, 58
Group sex, 153

Hackensmith, C. W., 96
Hale, Creighton, 71-72
Hampson, John L., 172, 173
Hart, Marie, 45
Harvard University, 91
Hawley, Adelaide, 98-99
Haworth, N.J., 73
Hearts, 58-59, 65
Hein, Fred V., 51-52
Hercules, 120
Hermaphrodites, 60-61, 171-72
Hernandez, Angela, 127
Herodotus, 124
Hillary, Edmund, 112
Hines, James, 87
Hippolyte, 120
History of Physical Education, 97
Hitchcock, Alfred, 151
Homosexuality, 132, 142
Hormones, 59-60, 65, 169-71
Horner, Matina, 19
Horney, Karen, 128, 147
Horses, riding, 142. *See also* Jockeys
Houston Oilers, 109
Howie, Carol, 108
Hoyt, Dicksie Ann, 58
Hunt, H. L., 109
Hunting, 63-64, 168. *See also* Amazons
Hurok, Sol, 50

Illinois, University of, 82

Index

Income, 29-30
Indiana, University of, 190
Institute for the Study of Sport and Society, 190

Jackson, Marjorie, 87
Jacobson, Pay Kelly, 85-86
Jahn, Friedrich, 96
Jockeys, 74-75, 76-77. *See also* specific riders
John Chrysostom, St., 134
Johns Hopkins University, 171-172
Johnson, Nan, 50
Johnson, Shirley, 83
Jong, Erica, 15
Journal of the American Medical Association, 57
Judo, 156-57
Jung, Carl, 143-45, 147

K-2 Plus Shirt Contest, 53
Kagan, Spencer, 104
Kaine, Elinor, 108
Kane, John, 20
Kapp, Rebecca, 48
Katz, Dave, 83
Kikuyus, 63
King, Billie Jean, 75
King, Carolyn, 191
King, Micki, 77
Klafs, Carl E., 61
Kleid, Terry, 48
Knox, John, 134
Korbut, Olga, 49
Koryak, the, 129
Kostric, Walter, 61, 64
Kozelka, Robert, 21, 22
Kraker, Francie, 39
Kurkjian, Ann Desantis, 159
Kusner, Kathy, 77

Lake Champlain, 69
Lake George, 67
Lake Michigan, swim across from Chicago to Benton Harbor, 68
Land, Edwin, 105, 111
Lane, Lois (character), 79
Latif Abo Heif, Abdel, 68-69
Lawrenson, Helen, 161, 163, 168
Le Mans, 104
Life, 105, 111

Lippincott, Helen, 107-8
Little League, 47, 71-72, 76, 191
Lombardi, Vince, 100, 106
Los Angeles Times, 83
Louvre, The, 198-99
Lung cancer, 29
Lungs, 59
Luther, Martin, 134

Maccoby, Eleanor, 69
McCord, James W., 103-4
Madden, John, 108
Madness. *See* Mental illness
Mage, Judy, 18-19, 77-78
Mailer, Norman, 149ff.
Maine, University of, 83-84
Malays, 63
Malaysia, 129
Man and Woman, Boy and Girl, 172
Manipulated Man, The, 44, 177
Manitoba Free Press, 94
Mann, Carol, 84
Marcotte, Dan, 106
Marston, William, 126
Marymount College, 189
Maslow, Abraham, 35, 147
Masochism, 150ff.
Massachusetts Institute of Technology (MIT), 190
Mead, Margaret, 18, 163, 166-67, 173
Mecom, John, 109
Meggyesy, Dave, 102-3
Melanion, 122
Men in Groups, 166
Meng, Heinz, 169
Menstruation, 64-65, 170, 171
Mental illness (madness), 27ff., 135, 137-49, 170
Merritt, Helen, 37
Metropolitan Golf Tournament, 73
Metropolitan Museum of Art, 116, 200
Miami Dolphins, 108
Michener, James, 133
Michigan, 191
Michigan, University of, 19, 103
Militarism, 102-3. *See also* War
Mimicry, 23
Mississippi, University of, 82
Mitchell, Elizabeth, 93
Mod Squad, 79
Moffo, Anna, 51

Money, John, 172-73
Money, 29-30 (*See also* Scholarships);
	prize, 72-73
Money Game, The (Smith), 15
Monkeys. *See* Primates
Montagu, Ashley, 163
Montler, Mike, 106
Morgan, Elaine, 164, 165-66
Morris, Desmond, 164-65
Morris, Jeannie, 108
Motherhood, 169, 181-82. *See also* Preg-
	nancy
Movies, 151-52
Ms., 15, 19
Murchison, Clint, 109
Murder, 151, 152
Muscle, 57, 60, 61. *See also* Strength
Musicians, 33-34. *See also* Singers
My World and Welcome to It, 17-18
Myths, 22, 145-47. *See also* Amazons

Namath, Joe, 105
Natan, Alex, 104
National Council on Alcoholism, 29
National Education Association, 79, 189
National Institute of Mental Health, 29
National Little League. *See* Little League
National Observer, 106
National Organization for Women
	(NOW), 53; Sports and Athletics
	Workshop, 193-95
National Recreation Congress, 98
New Chastity, The, 177
New England Patriots, 106
New Jersey Interscholastic Athletic
	Association, 81
New Orleans Saints, 109
New York, 144, 191 (*See also* Metropoli-
	tan Museum of Art); swim around
	Manhattan, 67-68
New York, State University of, at Cort-
	land, 82
New York Giants, 106
New York Mets, 105
New York State, 189
New York Times, 36, 46, 74, 89-90, 98,
	161 (*See also* specific reporters, sub-
	jects); *Book Review*, 89
New York Women's Professional Foot-
	ball Team, 48
New Yorker, The, 41
Nicaragua, 63-64

Niebelungenlied, 122
Nigeria, 104
Nison, L., 104
Nixon, Richard, 103
NOW. *See* National Organization for
	Women
Noyes' Modern Clinical Psychiatry, 139,
	146

Oakland Raiders, 108
Oberlin College, 190
Oedipus, 145-46
Office of Education, U.S., 79
Oldfield, Barney, 94
Olympics, 53, 67, 72, 74, 97, 126; ancient
	Greek, 90, 131; chromosome check
	at, 60-61; menstruation and victories,
	64; Pentathlon, 45, 46; pregnancy and
	victories, 65; running records, 87;
	woman expelled for sexual miscon-
	duct, 74
Onassis, Jacqueline, 185
Orcutt, Maureen, 73
Orestes, 160
Out of Their League, 102-3
Outing magazine, 95

Palmer, Sue, 81
Paracelsus, 134-35
Parents, 78, 146
Parr, Jean, 108
Parrish, Bernie, 109-10
Peleus, 123
Penis envy, 138-39
Penn State University conference, 23,
	58, 59
Penthesileia, 120-21
Pepe, Maria, 76
Perkins, Tony, 151
Pett, Saul, 103
Philadelphia Inquirer, 81
Pilbeam, David, 63, 167-68
Physical ability. *See* Strength
Physical activity. *See* Exercise
Piccard, Jean F., 113
Piccard, Jeannette, 113
Pindar, 123
Pitou, Penny, 53
Plato, 131
Plutarch, 120
Pollack, Bruglinde, 46
Pool halls, 186-87

Poole, Sharon, 76
Portz, Eileen, 79
Power, 183-86
Pregnancy, 64, 65-66
Press, the, 107-9
Press boxes, 107-8
Primates (apes), 59, 167, 169
Prison, mock, 180
Prostitution, 132, 152, 153
Proverbs 31, 133
Psychiatry, 135, 137-49, 153
Psycho (movie), 151
Psychoanalytic Quarterly, 150
Psychology Today, 61, 104, 112
Psychology of Woman, The. See Deutsch,
    Helene
Purr, Baby, Purr, 177-78

Racing. *See* Drivers and driving; Flying;
    etc.
Radcliffe College, 19, 189
Rape, 149ff.
Reich, Wilhelm, 147-48
Reichenau, General von, 96
Remits, Ernest, 111
Rheingold, Joseph, 140
Rice, Grantland, 100
Rich, Buddy, 32
Richards, Marilyn, 159
Ridgewood, N.J., 73
Rigby, Kathy, 49
Riggs, Bobby, 75-76
Rippon, Diane Struble, 67-69
Roberts, John, 20ff.
Rowing, 189-90. *See also* Boats and sail-
    ing
Rubenstein, Boris B., 64-65
Rudolph, Wilma, 87
Runners and running, 67, 87-88, 191. *See
    also* specific runners
Ruppert, Linda, 80-81
Russia and Russians (Soviets), 65, 125-26
    (*See also* specific athletes); Siberia, 129

Sadism, 150ff.
Sailing. *See* Boats and sailing
Sakol, Jeannie, 177-78
Salter, Stephanie, 108-9
San Bernardino, Calif., 81
San Francisco, 144; Candlestick Park,
    107-8
San Diego City College, 81

Sawyer, Tom, 82
Schauler, Eileen, 338
Schoenstein, Ralph, 71, 75, 76, 87-88
Scholarships, 189
Scott, Blanche, 94-95
Scott, Jack, 46, 47, 77, 106-7, 190
Scott, John, 59
Scott, Micki, 84, 85, 190
Scott-Maxwell, Florida, 24
Scythians, 124-25
Seaman, Barbara, 170
Sears, Eleanor, 90
Second Sex, The, 77
Secret Power of Femininity, The, 43
Seldin, Abbey, 81
Self-defense, 156
Seltman, Charles, 126-27ff.
Sempier, Evelyn Ay, 48
Seneca Falls Women's Rights Conven-
    tion, 91
Seventeen, 71, 75, 88
Sexual activity, 42-43, 132, 152-53, 165;
    rape, 149ff.; woman expelled from
    Olympics for misconduct, 74
Shaw, George Bernard, 183
Sherman, Julia, 62-63
Siberia, 129
Sichting, Fran, 189
Silverman, Al, 76
Singers, 37, 50-51
Skiing, 53. *See also* specific skiers
"Smith, Adam," 15
Smith, Elinor, 95
Smith, Robyn, 48, 74, 76-77
Smith College, 92
Smoking, 29
Smyrnaeus, Quintus, 115
Solanis, Valerie, 178
Source, The (Michener), 133
South Africa, 104
South America, 104-5
Soviets. *See* Russia and Russians
Spain, 127
Sparta and Spartans, 127-28, 129-30
Spatial orientation, 62-63
Sport: A Philosophic Inquiry, 55, 56
Sports, 19-20, 31-32ff., 45-54, 71-88,
    100-13, 186-87ff. (*See also* specific
    athletes, sports); in early part of cen-
    tury, 89-90ff.; female physique and,
    57-58ff.
Sports Illustrated, 47, 108

Sportscasting, 108
Stanton, Elizabeth Cady, 93
Startup, Maurine and Elbert, 43
Steinem, Gloria, 137, 184-85
Stern, Curt, 125
Strabo, 118, 119
Strati, Joan, 62
Strength (physical ability), 31-39, 55-69, 85-86, 184; developing, 156-60 (*See also* Exercise)
Sullivan, Victoria, 151-52, 155
Superman, 79
Supreme Court, 110
Sutton, May, 90
Sutton-Smith, Brian, 20ff.
Swimming, 67-69, 73, 82, 85-86. See also specific swimmers

Taming of the Shrew, The, 22
Taraldsen, Earl, 125-26
Tchambulian culture, 167
Teaneck, N.J., 81
Television, 78-79; sportscasters, 108
Tennis, 75-76, 80-81, 81-82, 189. See also specific players
Tennyson, Alfred Lord, 112
Terhune, Terry, 111
Tertullian, 134
Testosterone, 169-70
Textbooks, 79
Theogenes, 90
Thetis, 122-23
They Call It a Game, 109-10
Thomas, Clayton, 64
Thomas Aquinas, St., 134
Tiger, Lionel, 166
Time, 49, 75, 149, 189
Today's Health, 189
Todd, John, 91-92
"Tomboy," use of term, 93
Towers, Constance, 51
Track. *See* Runners and running
True, 48, 113
Turner, Clara Mae, 50-51
Turner's syndrome, 171, 172
Tyus, Wyomia, 87

"Ulysses" (Tennyson), 112
Unger, Rhoda K., 169

Van Buren, Abigail, 154
Van Horn, Louise, 47

Van Kiekebelt, Deborah, 46, 64
Vassar College, 92
Vatican, The, 200-1
Vichy, Women's Athletic Congress in, 97-98
Vietnam, 103
Vilar, Esther, 44, 177, 178
Violence, 149ff., 170, 178. See also Aggressiveness and aggression

Wagner, Richard, 122
Walker, Nicolette Milnes, 112
War, 90, 91. 96
Warhol, Andy, 178
Watergate, 104
Weiner, Jay, 88
Weiss, Paul, 55, 56, 69, 86-87
Wellesley College, 190
Wesleyan University, 190
Western Illinois University, 84
Western Michigan University, 83
Western women, 92-93
White, Marilyn, 82
Whitworth, Kathy, 47, 73
Wife-beating, 149, 152, 156
Wilson, June, 32
Wilson, Rita, 48
Wisconsin, University of, 92
Women in Antiquity. See Seltman, Charles
Women and Madness. See Chesler, Phyllis
Women's National Regatta, 190
Women's Rescue League of America, 94
Women's Transcontinental Air Race, 141
Wonder Woman, 126
Wood, Terry, 80
Woodhouse, Bobby, 74-75
Woodstock festival, 152-53
Working women, 29-30
World Sports Foundation for the Modernization of Sport, 190
World War I, 91, 96
Wrestling, 158, 188

Xenophon, 130, 131

Yale University, 190
Yannuzzi, Barbara, 38
Ypsilanti, Mich., 191

Zeus, 117, 118, 122
Zimbardo, Philip G., 180